LOVE AND INTIMACY

Love and Intimacy

Five Ways to Get Together and Stay Together

Joseph W. Walker III

Abingdon Press

Nashville

LOVE AND INTIMACY
FIVE WAYS TO GET TOGETHER AND STAY TOGETHER

This book is printed on acid-free paper.

Library of Congress Cataloging-in-Publication Data

Walker, Joseph Warren, 1967-
    Love and intimacy : five ways to get together and stay together / Joseph W. Walker III.
    p. cm.
    ISBN 978-1-4267-0404-8 (pbk. : alk. paper)
    1. Man-woman relationships—Religious aspects—Christianity. 2. Dating (Social customs)—Religious aspects—Christianity. 3. Marriage—Religious aspects—Christianity. I. Title.
    BT705.8.W35 2010
    241'.6765—dc22

                                                                                2009038225

10 11 12 13 14 15 16 17 18 19—10 9 8 7 6 5 4 3 2 1
MANUFACTURED IN THE UNITED STATES OF AMERICA

CONTENTS

ACKNOWLEDGMENTS

I am convinced that life is the best teacher of all. Also, those persons who have graced our lives with incredible insight are invaluable. What I have learned about relationships has primarily come from my mother. She imparted truths into my life early on that helped guide me as I navigated through the challenges of human relationships. Thank you, Rosa Walker, for being to me what Solomon's mother was to him—a voice! To my father, Joseph Walker Jr., who gave me the wisdom of self-reflection and an unwavering determination to pursue truth, I am blessed to carry your name. To all my family, I love you.

To my pastor, Dr. Harry Blake, I thank you for teaching me to pray without ceasing. Your spirit of compassion has taught me so much. To Bishop Paul Morton, thank you for teaching me the value of integrity in high places.

Thanks to the Mount Zion Baptist Church of Nashville, Tennessee. You guys are amazing. Your questions sparked much of the content of this book. Thank you for your support and prayers. I remain convinced that I pastor the greatest church in the world.

Last but not least, to my wonderful wife. I am so blessed to be married to such an amazing and supportive woman. Stephaine, thank you for allowing me the space to be creative and produce the vision God has given to me for the world. I am convinced our love represents God bringing two people together. Your love teaches me to love better every day.

To God be the Glory for the things God has done!

STRAIGHT TALK FROM ME TO YOU

A long-lasting, loving, intimate relationship is a beautiful thing. I should know because I've been blessed with two. The day I married Dr. Diane Greer was one of the happiest days of my life. It was filled with great expectation. We both looked forward to spending the rest of our lives together, but that did not happen because Diane died a few years later. For a long time I thought I would never again experience that kind of real, steadfast love. I even thought perhaps God did not mean for me to marry again. I should have trusted God. I should have known that He understood my pain and would not leave me there. This past year I married Dr. Stephaine Hale. It was a day I will never forget. God gave me the desires of my heart and proved to me that He is a restorer. I will never forget how she looked coming down the aisle. I remain convinced that that day began the best days of the rest of my life. As we continue to live, work, and love, we also know that our relationship will be successful and satisfying as long as God is in the center of our lives.

Because I've been there, I also know that relationships take work. They don't just happen. They are give-and-take propositions. Sometimes I give more; sometimes she takes more. Sometimes I take more; sometimes she gives more. That's the way it goes. But after all the fluff is brushed away, there are five basic steps in this journey of getting together and staying together: it all comes down to these.

This book is meant to be straight talk from me to you. I won't pull any punches. I won't sugarcoat what needs to be said. Intimate relationships are too important for anything less. I'm going to be as real as I can be, I'm going to set high standards and know my boundaries and limits, because I'm on your team. I want, no, God wants you to have lasting love. And if you follow these steps, you will find it.

THE HOLY HOOKUP

A friend told me, "Walker, man, I got this convertible. It's an old car, an antique I'm fixing up. The strangest thing happened! My car stopped and I thought something terrible had happened, but it was the gas indicator light. But guess where it broke?" I said, "Where, Doc?" "It broke on full," he said. "It's the strangest thing. I'm driving my car and my gas indicator says full, whether there's gas in the tank or not. I'm in the car with people riding with me asking me why I'm pulling up to the gas station when it seems I have a full tank of gas. But they don't know that the fuel indicator is broken. I know that with this car, you can't go on what you see. I know when my car really needs to be filled up."

The same is true when you're looking to hook up with people. You're looking at someone wearing an Armani suit, Via

Spiga shoes; they sport Prada and Gucci and they think they got it going on. You think they got it going on too. But some of these folk have broken parts. They look like they're full—large and in charge; but in reality they are broken, empty—like my friend's car with the perpetrating fuel indicator. You've got to check out what's on the inside, because not everything that looks good on the outside is filled with the Spirit on the inside!

A holy relationship begins with two whole people, not two unhealthy, needy ones. There can be no relationship without a man and a woman—whole and constantly growing toward greater wholeness. Until we as individuals understand who, where, and whose we are, no attempt at a healthy relationship with anybody will be successful. Before I am qualified to be in relationship with someone else, I have to seek to be whole within myself. Only then can I truly give myself to another and receive love from another.

You see people who prowl around for love, seeking a relationship out of their deficiencies. You may see them at happy hour, at the club, even at church. They are on the hunt for someone, anyone to be with. For them it's all about how they're dressed, the rap they bring, how they carry themselves—superficials. They have an emptiness to fill; they are needy. They want somebody to complete them, to plug up their holes and fill their gaps. This kind of person can never be in a truly satisfying relationship. Relationships are give and take. Prowlers only take. They can't give. Relationship prowlers want you because of what you can do for them, not what they can do for you.

So before you step out that door in your fine attract-a-guy, pull-a-girl attire, how about delving inside yourself to present as excellent a picture on the inside as on the outside? It takes an open mind, a receptive heart, and a little faith and trust in the One who made you.

BIBLICAL BLUEPRINT FOR RELATIONSHIPS

The biblical blueprint on relationships is being overlooked by a world filled with its own righteousness. For some years, same-sex marriage has been near or at the top of any list of leading religious, secular, political controversies. In this country, states either allow same-sex marriage or ban it. One argument for same-sex marriages is that, considering the fact that over 50 percent of marriages end in divorce, there's no proof that traditional families enhance our society. This issue is complex and divisive. It's easy to criticize and I don't believe states that condone same-sex marriage are right. But it's important for us to realize that we really can't criticize if we don't have credibility.

Too many people are getting into relationships with people who are not on their spiritual level. Many folk are dating on the rebound and marrying too soon. Others are marrying too quickly because they just want to have a husband or a wife. Today divorce is an easy option for when things get tough. We now know that a divorce affects a child for thirty years.[1] That eight-year-old child of divorced parents doesn't come to grips with the separation until age 38! We're spending countless dollars on elaborate weddings but investing nothing in maintaining marriages.

We're letting people hook us up with people they think we ought to be with and we're ending up in some crazy relationships. Rather than depending on God's blueprint

> A holy hookup is a relationship between a man and a woman founded on biblical principles, intended to glorify God and live out God's purpose for the two people who have become one flesh.

for marriage, we're being guided by unreliable and unrealistic influences. People are letting hormones take over their ability to reason. People who don't know how to live single, saved, and sanctified lives are moving too quickly into untested, unrealistic, unblessed relationships. Rather than having holy hookups, we got some hellish hookups.

There is a principle in the Bible called the law of primary reference. It means if you want to know where God stands on a thing, go back to see how God did it in the beginning. So when we look at Adam and Eve, we get a great model of what God intended for healthy relationships and healthy marriages. A holy hookup is a relationship between a man and a woman founded on biblical principles, intended to glorify God and live out God's purpose for the two people who have become one flesh.

SPIRITUAL SURGERY

For a holy hookup preparation is critical. God has to perform spiritual surgery on you in order for you to get this hookup, to bring forth relationship. God says you need to be ready and need spiritual surgery. Here is what I mean by spiritual surgery.

The LORD God caused a deep sleep to fall on Adam, and he slept; and He took one of his ribs, and closed up the flesh in its place. Then the rib which the LORD God had taken from man
    He made into a woman, and He brought her to the man. And Adam said,
        "This is now bone of my bones
        and flesh of my flesh;
        she shall be called Woman,
        because she was taken out of Man."
(Genesis 2:21-23)

God opened Adam's body, took something out, and closed his flesh. When God performs this procedure, it is major surgery, not an outpatient procedure. Many of us treat relationships and marriage like a minor procedure. That's why people are in and out of relationships.

IDENTIFICATION

Surgery requires many intricate steps. Every patient who goes through surgery has to have a pre-op examination. It is part of the preparation process before the surgery. The first period of a pre-op exam, identification, happens when the medical team gets a patient's brief history to make sure the hospital has the right person. One of the worst things that can happen is performing surgery on the wrong patient.

With the holy hookup, the process of identification is spiritual, performed by the Perfect One. God is not going to give you something He has for somebody else. God won't give somebody else what He has for you.

POSITIONING

The next step in preparing a patient for surgery is positioning. This is an examination to ensure that the patient is positioned safely on the operating table to endure the various surgical procedures and that the equipment needed to perform those procedures is aligned for the patient's ultimate safety. In a relationship, you can't date people who are not in position. This person has to be in a specific position and have a certain posture for God to work on them. When you're looking for hookups in the clubs or placing ads on the Internet ("Brown chocolate looking for strawberry supreme"), you are not in a safe position for surgery. The reason some relationships are strange and marriages are messed up is because people won't get in position for God to work on them.

STERILIZATION

Once the person makes it through positioning, the sterilization process begins. The space where the surgery will take place is cleaned and sterilized so the patient and the surgical area are not infected. The reason some people can't get in healthy relationships is because their lives are still contaminated with sin, resulting from unhealthy choices. God says, "I got to clean you up. I got to purify you." What can wash away my sin? Nothing but the blood of Jesus! God's got some Ajax for your attitude, some Lysol for your lifestyle.

God made people in His image. The biggest mistake one can make is connecting with somebody who is not in the image of the Father. When you are considering dating somebody, you have to ask yourself: Does this person love God?

Is she saved? Does she have a healthy relationship with God? Does she go to church voluntarily? If not, then you petition God for the holy hookup.

One of the worst ways to insult a father is to tell him his child doesn't look like him. That is a major insult. But when you're looking for someone to hook up with for life, you have to examine the person against God's image. When you look at this person, you've got to ask: Does he look like the Father? In his walk and talk, does he reflect the image of the Father?

"And the LORD God formed man of the dust of the ground, and breathed into his nostrils the breath of life; and man became a living being" (Genesis 2:7). Here is the breath of God. Not only is a righteous person in the image of God, but the righteous person is filled with the Spirit. We need people in our lives who are full of the Spirit and not full of everything else, people who are guided by and submitted to the Spirit of God, not the flesh. Too often we hook up with people based on what's on the outside and miss the blessing that God intended for us to see on the inside.

PROVIDENTIAL CONNECTION

The LORD God said, "It is not good for the man to be alone. I will make a helper suitable for him."

Now the LORD God had formed out of the ground all the beasts of the field and all the birds of the air. He brought them to the man to see what he would name them; and whatever the man called each living creature, that was its name. So the man gave names to all the livestock, the birds of the air and all the beasts of the field.

> But for Adam no suitable helper was found. So the
> LORD God caused the man to fall into a deep sleep; and
> while he was sleeping, he took one of the man's ribs and
> closed up the place with flesh. Then the LORD God made
> a woman from the rib he had taken out of the man, and
> he brought her to the man.
> The man said,
> > "This is now bone of my bones
> > and flesh of my flesh;
> > she shall be called 'woman,'
> > for she was taken out of man."
> For this reason a man will leave his father and mother
> and be united to his wife, and they will become one flesh.
> (Genesis 2:18-24 NIV)

After the preparation stage, the next stage for the holy
hookup is the providential connection, how God's going to
work this thing out. God begins the process of hooking
this relationship up. Now, in Genesis 2:18, God plans to make
a helpmeet suitable for Adam. God says, "It's time to hook
it up."

Out of the ground the Lord formed every beast of the field
and every bird in the air. He brought them to Adam to see
what Adam would call them. Sometimes God tells you when
it's your season. You know it's your time because you've got
your stuff together. You also understand that the very first
being who shows up after that promise may not be the blessing; it may be some beast. God may show you beasts and
birds, let you examine them, so when you get the ultimate
blessing, you will appreciate what you get.

The Bible said Adam found nothing suitable for him.
Maybe God is waiting for you to examine and label all the
friendships/relationships so that you will let go and let Him

step in and do what you cannot do. God caused a deep sleep to fall upon Adam and performed spiritual anesthesia. This is major surgery. God was saying, "Adam, you tried to do it your way, now let me do it. In order for me to do this, I need you to rest in me now."

God tells us to sit down somewhere and rest in Him! I know some people say, "But you don't understand. My biological clock is ticking. I got nobody in my life. I had my life all planned out and I was supposed to be here about 25, have this at age 28, and have that at age 32." While you're comparing your goals to your age, someone who's married is saying, "I wish I had rested in God." With a providential connection comes the revelation that this beast/bird is not for me. I'm resting in God, I'm waiting on God to do it. Strength will rise if I wait upon the Lord.

COVENANT OF PRAISE

The final thing the text gives us is that when God hooks this relationship up, it becomes a covenant of praise. When you get to this point, you understand the power of the praise covenant. A covenant is an agreement between two parties; it simply suggests that there is reciprocity. There has to be a connection, a partnership; a sense that we both share and we both give. You cannot be in a relationship or a marriage when it's you only. If you're the only one giving and pouring out, there is no relationship; there is no marriage. You are by yourself. The holy hookup, the ultimate relationship, is a two-way street and it brings glory to God's name. The response of two people joined by God's spiritual guidelines answers the eternal quest for compatibility. This hookup/connection produces two people who together are a union that praises and lives for God, who become co-creators with God, and who become a sanctuary for God's kingdom.

> God caused the man to fall into a deep sleep; and while he was sleeping, he took one of the man's ribs and closed up the place with flesh. (Genesis 2:21 NIV)

Here's the covenant of praise: A man leaves his father and mother and embraces his wife and they become one flesh. He says: I appreciate you, Mama, but I got to go. Daddy, holler! I got a wife now. I got a new family, in-laws ain't about to mess this up. I got to take care of this gift. The Bible said that they—husband and wife—were naked and not ashamed. That's because they were into each other and they had no secrets; they could be open and honest with each other about their strengths and their weaknesses.

WHO IS YOUR ONE RIB?

Someone asked, "Bishop, does God give you just one extra rib per life?" I said, "Well, because we are free-born agents, we could have as many ribs as we want to have. But according to God's word, God gives one rib." The person continued: "Well, who's the one rib?" I said, "Name the one person God put on this earth to put up with you. Who's the one person who will accept your flaws as well as your talents, stands up for you and picks up behind you; the one who offers you forgiveness and understanding, the one person in the whole wide world who will put up with your trifling self."

STRAIGHT TALK FOR MEN

Now, men, I want you to understand something: we're the covering; spiritually, we are the head. This title is an honor that cannot be abused and a responsibility to be regarded seriously. Too many men want to cover, to be the head, but they aren't in covenant—with God, with their mate, or with themselves. They are doing nothing to be the head.

To covenant involves a two-way connection. The man has got to do something to be the head. He has to love that wife like Christ loved the church. That's covenant. When he understands the God-inspired concept of head of the family, and accepts that position, he should be the head. If he can understand that, then he has to take responsibility for this position.

STRAIGHT TALK FOR WOMEN

In order for the woman to be everything that she is supposed to be, God had to take something out of the man. The woman would have never been all she was supposed to be unless God took something out of the man. That's why you have to say, "Lord, whatever you need to take out, whatever's got to come out, take it out now!" From the rib that the Lord took from man, He made a woman, and presented the woman to the man. He made her a present, a gift. Sisters, you need to see yourself as a gift from God to men. It's right there in the Scripture. You are a present; you should be treasured and treated as such.

ONLY GOD PERFORMS THE HOLY HOOKUP

God made the man anthropomorphically, physically first. But God put the spirit of the woman inside the man. So all of Adam's life he knew there was something connected to him.

When God took the rib out, He released the spirit of the woman and built the woman from the rib. He released the woman's spirit from the man and then, the Bible says, He closed the flesh back up, so no other woman could get in.

So after God performed surgery, Adam woke up. Adam knew that she came from him because his first words to Eve were: "You are bone of my bone, flesh of my flesh, you shall be called woman because you are taken out of man." He knew immediately that she was the one. They didn't have a formal introduction. He could sense that she came from him. When God makes the holy hookup surgery for us and we meet our mate, we know—sometimes immediately, sometimes much later—but we know. We have the same goals, the same visions, similar responses to circumstances, compatible concerns.

That energy, that compatibility, is a beautiful thing. Something may be going on in my heart and I wonder how you know something's going on. It's because you came from me. I could never hurt you, because to harm you is to harm me because we are one flesh. For me to talk bad about you is like me talking bad about myself. When this holy hookup took place, Adam's words were intimate: You are part of me.

> **Most men only understand intimacy from the outside in. We try to touch you on the outside to get on the inside. But a woman says, "No, intimacy has to be on the inside of me. Intimacy means you are in-to-me-to-see."**

I love you for what's on the inside of you. This is intimacy from the inside out.

Most men only understand intimacy from the outside in. We try to touch you on the outside to get on the inside. But a woman says, "No, intimacy has to be on the inside of me. Intimacy means you are in-to-me-to-see. If you could just get in to me to really see who I am, you'd understand. I'm more than these jeans."

IT IS NEVER TOO LATE

Marriage is a ministry and ministry means meeting needs. If you didn't do it right, it's not too late for surgery, for a providential connection. Fight for your marriage. Protect your marriage. Pray for your marriage. This is major surgery. Whatever isn't right in your marriage, get still and rest in God; do the preparation for the spiritual surgery; pray together often, and watch God perform the holy hookup. After surgery, you and your mate will have the rewards of resting in God's will and realizing the redemptive miracle of new life in God.

A PERSONAL WORD FOR YOU

God wants you to be blessed. You have God's guarantee and, for what it's worth, you have mine as well.

> Blessed are those who trust in the LORD
> and have made the LORD their hope and confidence.
> They are like trees planted along a riverbank,
> with roots that reach deep into the water.
> Such trees are not bothered by the heat
> or worried by long months of drought.
> Their leaves stay green,
> and they never stop producing fruit.
> (Jeremiah 17:7-8 NLT)

NOTE

1. One longitudinal study tracked children whose parents divorced in 1946 and tested them two and three decades later. Even thirty years after the divorce, negative long-term effects were clearly present in the income, health, and behavior of many of the grown offspring. Australian House of Representatives Standing Committee on Legal and Constitutional Affairs, *To Have and to Hold*, 35–36 (1998).

BE READY FOR A HOLY HOOKUP

TRUST THE TRUTH

Eli peered fearfully through the window. Was she coming yet? If only she wouldn't come until he remembered what he had promised her. He knew it had something to do with where he was supposed to take her, but when you date three girls at one time, it's hard to keep all the details straight.

Evon hated kids, but she loved Tim, who happened to be bringing his young son to meet her tonight. If things worked out, they all would go away to the mountains next weekend. Just great! Why, she wondered to herself, had she told Tim that she adored children and sure, she'd love to spend time with his little boy. Actually she never got along with children, had nothing in common with them, and was dreading the whole thing.

To be ready to get together, we first have to trust that telling the truth is the best way. Have you ever told a lie or kept a secret so that other people would like you? We probably all have. When we meet a person we'd really like to get close to, sometimes we are tempted to suppress certain things, usually unresolved issues, mistakes, or character flaws. It's natural. Everyone wants to make a good impression. Sometime we are even afraid that once they know these things they might not like or want to be with us. But in not unveiling those things in an appropriate way, you create a misrepresentation and problems down the road.

When we enter into relationships under false pretenses, suppressing the real us, others can fall in love with the person we created and not the real us. And because we know it is a false representation, we always are on guard, afraid to let something slip. Later reality sets in and things start leaking out. They learn that we've been keeping secrets, and they begin to wonder and doubt the relationship. If you want to be ready to enter into a relationship, you first have to let the truth be your friend.

FULL DISCLOSURE

When God matchmakes, there is full disclosure. Because you are aligned with the truth, you know God accepts you and that you are on the road toward healing and wholeness. When you approach a new relationship, you are secure enough to disclose up front any negative or positive things that have occurred in your life. You know you've grown from your mistakes and used those lessons to groom you to be a better person. You can freely admit mistakes and lessons you've learned because of God's acceptance, grace, and mercy toward you. You can admit struggles that you still deal with and share how you've been delivered.

When you're honest at the beginning of a relationship, other people know they can take you or leave you. They know what they are getting. If you really care about someone, doesn't that person deserve the option of saying no? How would it feel to be married to somebody for years, waking up in the same bed, eating at the same table, having children together, and then having the marriage fall apart because your mate believed that she never really knew you? I'd feel betrayed, hurt, and angry. Take the honest and godly road. If someone decides to pass on you, it may hurt initially; but it will also tell you that this relationship would not have worked out anyway.

DISCOVER YOUR SPIRITUAL IDENTITY

To be ready for a meaningful relationship you have to know who you are. In many ways you and I both are a collage of experiences. Some of these experiences bless us and make us happy and other experiences curse us and make us bleed. The key to knowing who we are is understanding who we are to God. That way we can be confident in our own skin. When you know who you are in God, you will know the truth and the truth will set you free for full disclosure.

It's God's style to create with many complex and interesting aspects. That's why there are more than a thousand varieties of bananas and millions of different flowers and fish. There are even hundreds of thousands of different beetles, many uniquely suited for a single plant. Humans are also multifaceted. You are complex and interesting. The Bible says that you are wonderfully made. You are worthy because God created a unique, special you. That's just the way God rolls.

THE TRUE YOU

Who is the true you? Who is the person that God calls you to be? The person that God can help you become?

YOU ARE ACCEPTED

Who are you? You are accepted by God. In John 15:15 Jesus calls His disciples His friends. As a modern-day follower of Jesus, you are a friend of Christ, accepted by Christ. "But to all who believed him and accepted him, he gave the right to become children of God" (John 1:12 NLT). Jesus' recognition of the woman with the issue of blood showed His acceptance of her. He saw through the crowds, through the cultural expectations, through physical disabilities, and validated her and her faith. He accepted her and He accepts us, wounds and all.

YOU ARE JUSTIFIED

But just because God accepts you, that does not mean that you are in a right relationship with Him now. God knows we just can't make it right by ourselves, so He justifies us. Romans 5:1 says, "Therefore, having been justified . . . we have peace with God." Don't let the failures in your life stop you from acting and living like you're God's child. Tell yourself: I am acquitted, I have peace with all. It is Just-As-If-I'd never done anything wrong. Then in 1 Corinthians 6:19-20, you learn that you've been "bought at a price." He thought enough of you to die for you. He did that for me too!

YOU ARE SECURE

This is a big one, because we have a generation of insecure people. Too much insecurity ruins relationships. Have you been a victim of somebody else's insecurity? Someone yells at you because he doesn't know what to do? Someone accuses you because she is afraid of getting caught for something she did? He takes something away from you because your having it makes him feel small? The insanity behind their paranoia can drive you nuts! One of the best things you can bring to a relationship is your secure personality. You are secure because you believe what God has done for you! Your security is not based on how anyone treats you, attends to you, or even loves you. You do not have to seek security in someone else because you are secure already.

Romans 8, verse 1 says, "There is therefore now no condemnation to them which are in Christ Jesus, who walk not after the flesh, but after the Spirit" (KJV). That means I'm secure because I'm free from condemnation. I may have a checkered past, but that's behind me. Condemnation can be deadly in relationships. It keeps people from telling the truth about who they really are and where they've really been. They're afraid you'll condemn them and hold it against them. If you've had a troubled past, you have to be secure in God's promise and say that *was* me; but now, I'm a new man in Christ Jesus, a new woman in Christ Jesus. Let people test you—you are steady and secure.

YOU ARE ANOINTED

Second Corinthians 1:21-22 reminds us that "it is God who establishes us with you in Christ and has anointed us, by putting his seal on us and giving us his Spirit in our hearts as a first installment" (NRSV). That tells me that God's got His hand on my life. I am one of the anointed. I'm not just walking around without purpose. I am confident in my anointing. And I can respect your confidence in your anointing.

YOU ARE PROTECTED

First John 5:18 explains that "We know that those who are born of God do not sin, but the one who was born of God protects them, and the evil one does not touch them" (NRSV). God's got my back, and I feel safe.

YOU ARE SIGNIFICANT

Listen, people of God: in Ephesians 2:10 the Bible says you are God's workmanship. "For we are what he has made us, created in Christ Jesus for good works, which God prepared beforehand to be our way of life" (NRSV). Look at how significant you are. God made you with a purpose. Your value is not decided by other people; your value is placed on you by God.

YOU ARE GOD'S TEMPLE

First Corinthians 3:16 says, "Don't you know that you yourselves are God's temple and that God's Spirit lives in you?" (NIV). Inside of you dwells the very power and presence of God. Please, don't think you mean nothing. You're valuable. If you're thinking, "I ain't nothing. I guess nobody wants to be me. I've been going to speed dating and they don't even come my way," who do you think you'll attract? If you talk like that, behave like that, even have posture like that, you won't attract anyone.

There is another meaning in this scripture as well. When Paul, the writer of 1 Corinthians, says that "you are God's temple," the word for "you" in the original Greek really means "you all." He means that together we are God's temple. We are meant to work and play together as a people of God. We are meant to be in relationship and help each other.

YOU ARE A FRUIT BEARER

"You did not choose Me, but I chose you and appointed you that you should go and bear fruit, and that your fruit should remain, that whatever you ask the Father in My name He may give you" (John 15:16). You bear much fruit in your life, inevitably, because of your relationship with Christ. This means you are productive; you are not fruit-less; you bring gifts and accomplishments into your relationship. This is a strong point in being relationship ready.

YOU ARE FEARFULLY AND WONDERFULLY MADE!

Put this verse on the refrigerator door or have it as part of your signature in your text and e-mail messages: "I praise you, for I am fearfully and wonderfully made. Wonderful are your works; that I know very well" (Psalm 139:14 NRSV). God took His time when He made you. God made your personality the way He wanted it to be. God put all these gifts inside of you. Your spiritual identity is God's statement about who you are. It is what God has done for you to make you whole.

One afternoon I was watching a football game. The quarterback launched an impossible throw. The running back made an impossible catch. The team scored and won the game. I cheered; it was so great. It was too wonderful for words. It was a fearsome, awesome play. When the Bible says that you are "fearfully" made, it does not mean that God wants you to live in fear or that other people should be afraid of you. It simply means that you are awesome. You are too valuable for words.

TRUST THE ONE WHO MADE YOU

So, before you step out that door in your fine attract-a-guy, pull-a-girl attire, how about delving inside yourself to present as excellent a picture on the inside as on the outside? It takes an open mind, a receptive heart, and faith and trust in the One who made you.

Here are some concrete ways to help you grow toward wholeness so you can be relationship ready when the time is right. They will help you move forward and overcome the obstacles that are blocking you from a healthy relationship.

1. CONSULT WITH GOD TO DEVELOP YOUR STANDARDS FOR RELATIONSHIPS

Start with God. Learn to trust Him. After my first wife died, it was hard for me to open up to anyone and harder still to trust. I just did not want to be hurt again. I should have known better, but I didn't. So I prayed and opened God's Word.

There are many kinds of relationships that challenge how well you know and understand people and yourself. Psalm 37:4 says, "Delight yourself . . . in the LORD"; in other words, be into God, be excited about God. One version of the Bible (*The Message*) says, "Keep company with GOD, / get in on the best." Be comfortable with just you and God; camp out with God, and "He shall give you the desires of your heart." Remind yourself of this blessing: "God wants me to have the true desires of my heart."

"He who walks with wise men will be wise, / But the companion of fools will be destroyed" (Proverbs 13:20). What I learn from this verse is that you have God's permission to be selective about the people in your life. Your values, your commitments, your purpose, and the path of your spiritual journey are influenced by the people who surround you. When you walk with fools, guess what's going to happen? Guess where you will end up?

As you are walking toward wholeness, you have to understand that people need to qualify for *your* approval. There are specific qualifications to meet *your* standards. Just as potential homeowners prepare and stretch to qualify for their homes, your potential mate has to qualify for you. You know that the value of the house determines how stringent the requirements of qualification are and how many

> **Be selective about the people in your life.**

> **The people you allow to step into and out of your life also show how much you value yourself.**

hoops you have to jump through just to get the house. The same is true for you. Whatever value you place on yourself will determine your standards about allowing people to step in and out of your life.

If someone is going to qualify for you, be ready to let them know (in a clear, assertive, positive way) what the requirements are, so they won't waste your time and you won't waste theirs. Let them know what you value and what you believe are the most excellent influences for your life's journey. Share your vision and where you perceive God is guiding you. Talk to them about your relationship with God and how important it is to you. That will give them the first clue about the qualifications they must bring. That's not arrogance, that's just truth. If they don't listen or ignore you, that is a clear signal that they are not right for you.

The most important time in your life to be picky, strict, and extremely selective is when you are considering a mate for life. In this case you are the underwriter for the loan (relationship) that they are trying to qualify for. It may take the person pursuing you a little longer to qualify because you are not interested in a short-term loan. **Say to yourself, "I'm expensive and I'm not apologizing for it! I am no cheap thrill. There's no rebate with this relationship."**

2. PROCESS THE PAIN OF YOUR PAST

Once you have opened the Word and begun to listen to God, you can be sure that God will have a plan for you. And an important part of His plan for you will be for you to face and process the pain of your past. It may be uncomfortable and it may even hurt, but like lancing a wound or getting a shot, the short-term pain is well worth the long-term benefit. Paul says in Philippians, "Beloved, I do not consider that I have made it my own; but this one thing I do: forgetting what lies behind and straining forward to what lies ahead, I press on toward the goal for the prize of the heavenly call of God in Christ Jesus" (Philippians 3:13-14 NRSV).

Processing and growing from the pain of your past means you have to embrace your future. Paul says I have to get to a point in my life where I have to acknowledge that I am an individual and I have had pain in my life. I cannot be in denial about what hurt me. Once I own my pain, I must then come to a place where I don't let my pain rob me of my future. This is what I mean. When you burn your finger while trying to light the grill, it really hurts. But the hurt will go away more quickly if you simply let it hurt and don't fight the pain. This may sound foolish, but it works. It takes energy to push the pain away, and fear of the pain actually makes the pain worse. But if you just accept the pain, it's like your body says, "OK, I am hurt. Now I can get on with the healing." But if you are truly afraid that experiencing the pain will destroy you, go find a trustworthy person to talk to about it.

Forgetting pain does not mean that I eradicate the memory of what happened. It means even though my memory of the pain is with me, I don't give the pain influence over my

current condition. I don't allow the pain to control my decisions about today. It means I do away with pain's power over
my entire self. Recent science says that every time you recall
a memory, you change it. If you recall a memory in the
context of a relationship of trust, the pain will not be as great
and healing can happen. That is why talking to a nonjudg-
mental friend or perhaps a pastor can help.

Learn from the pain. As I deal with my pain I have to learn
to draw wisdom from it. In every painful situation I can learn
something about myself as well
as about others. I don't eradicate it from memory, because
I use that memory to remind
me of that pain to teach me to
never go through that again.
It will not have influence on
my current condition.

Learn to draw wisdom from painful experiences.

Now I'm in a position to reach for the things that are
before me! I can embrace my future, consistently and confidently reaching for something greater for my life. I try never
to be apathetic or passive or fall into depression by saying, "I
don't have a reason to live because of the pain I've experienced." No! Pain never has to be the end of my story. I'm
still reaching for those things that God promised me! So my
position is that I thank God for the vision to see beyond my
pain. I'm reaching for whatever it is God promises me, but it's
not going to come easily. Jesus' crucifixion was not the end,
only the prelude to the Resurrection. God will resurrect our
life from pain as well and help press toward the goal line.

Pressing toward the goal also indicates a commitment to
not let this obstacle overtake me. It gives me the commit-

ment not to give up. It may mean that I have to overcome the naysayers and maybe even those doubts in my own head. With diligence, work, and the grace of God, I can develop patterns and habits that can help point me toward what God wants for my life.

One of the greatest enemies in pressing forward or reaching upward is guilt. But God helps us overcome guilt with grace. I cannot allow the guilt of bad decisions and the mess I got caught up in to paralyze me. The Bible says in 1 John 1:9, "If we confess our sins, He is faithful and just to forgive us our sins and to cleanse us from all unrighteousness." Everybody we meet will come with some past issues. The truth is that either those issues will be points of reference to help us get to the next level or they will paralyze us. Tell yourself: "I will not be paralyzed by my pain."

3. LET GO OF YOUR FEARS

After processing pain, you have to let go of your fears of future pain. How? Second Timothy 1:7 reminds us that we serve a God who "has not given us a spirit of fear, but of power and of love and of a sound mind." To let go of your fears, put your trust in something solid and unchanging: the faithfulness of God. God always makes good on His promise to be there for you. Psalm 23 says that God leads us and walks before, beside, and behind us. We are never without His ready help in time of trouble. If you are in a fear-based relationship, God isn't part of it, because God does not give us a spirit of fear!

What are our fears? Fear of being alone? Fear of being used? Fear of not being good enough? Into every relationship, we bring some of those fears, because we are human. But when we operate solely out of fear (or anxiety or anger), we make bad choices. Fear will make us move ahead of God's plan for our lives. Our anxiety about a person or experience causes us to focus so much on what we are afraid of that we miss out on God's guidance. We are so anxious listening for acceptance from another person that we can't hear God's voice. And sometimes we are so lust-driven that we don't hear anything at all. A wise man, Harry Stack Sullivan, said that anxiety cuts off foresight. That is to say, when we are afraid, we are unable to focus and think clearly. We only hear the fear talking, not God.

But some of us have a fear-based relationship with God. We can't have a good day without wondering, "Lord, what's going to happen? Something's getting ready to happen, 'cause the day's been too good. Why can't the day just be a good day?" Why can't we just give God glory that nothing bad happened? We're good at producing this fear! But do you know we have this promise in Psalm 84:11? If we trust in God, "No good thing does the Lord withhold from those who walk uprightly" (NRSV). God is not waiting behind some corner to trip us up. No, God is faithful, kind, and loving.

We can let go of our fears by walking in childlike grace before God. We need to stop walking in fear and walk in love, with a sound mind. We need to stop letting fear make us do crazy stuff! We've got to commit to the belief that God has a plan for each of us and boldly seek and receive that plan. Walk uprightly. God says no good thing will He withhold from you.

4. BE EQUALLY YOKED IN VALUES AND VISION

What does it mean to be yoked with someone? In the Gospel of Matthew, Jesus says, "Take my yoke upon you, and learn of me; for I am meek and lowly in heart: and ye shall find rest unto your souls. For my yoke is easy, and my burden is light" (Matthew 11:29-30 KJV). The word Jesus uses for "yoke" in this scripture means a training yoke, what was used to break in a young ox to help him learn to plow the field. When farmers wanted to train an inexperienced ox, they yoked him via the training yoke to a more experienced ox. To plow they walked side-by-side straight down the field. During training the experienced ox carried all the weight of the plow so all the other would have to do is walk. The older ox was really doing all the work. Soon the young ox would get distracted, impatient, or whatever; and he would try to veer off in some other direction. The training yoke was made so that when this happened it would rub the young ox's neck. To avoid the pain of a raw neck, the young ox quickly learned to walk beside the older ox. In time they came to share the burden equally. What Jesus means is that He will carry the weight; all we have to do is walk beside Him.

A great relationship examines and honors values and vision. To be equally yoked with someone means that you share the load equally and walk side-by-side with a common goal. When we share values and vision, we are equally yoked (2 Corinthians 6:14). We believe in the same things. You believe in and want to imitate Jesus Christ. So do I. We believe in going to church; we believe in sitting under the Word of God together. If I have to beg you to come to church, clearly we are not equally yoked. That's a deal breaker.

Sometimes people say to me, "Even though he/she doesn't go to church, he/she is still growing. They just need to see my example." That statement assumes you will save the other.

> **There is only one Messiah and it isn't you.**

Please understand: you are not the Messiah. Only Jesus is our Messiah. When we enter into relationships thinking we're gonna save this person, we are headed for disaster. We were never designed to save people. That is the job of the Savior of the world. Jesus died for us and it is His blood that redeems and saves—not you, your prayers, or your good intentions. I've seen too many people spend too much time and energy trying to corral persons into changing their values. It just does not work that way.

Here are two relationship questions you should always ask yourself: First, does the relationship honor God? When the relationship honors God, you see how others benefit from your relationship as the two of you serve together and seek God's will. Second, does your relationship bring you closer to God? Part of sharing your connection with God with another person means you spend time together in God's presence. You pray together and for each other; you have ongoing conversations about your spiritual walk and goals.

Vision is also about economics. Couples fight over money more than most everything else. Although you can't measure somebody based on how much money they make or don't make, being equally yoked in vision means the two of you share and are committed to the same sight or anticipate similar things. Having vision for your life means you not only have a job but are also seeking God's purpose and working toward honoring the gifts God has blessed you with. Vision means that you save the money you do have and use it to enhance that purpose and bring your vision into reality.

5. DEVELOP A DISCIPLINED LIFE

Let's be honest. A lot of us are out of control—sexually, financially, emotionally, physically, spiritually. So we are asking people to take on a lot to be in relationship with us. Romans 12:2 says, "And do not be conformed to this world, but be transformed by the renewing of your mind, that you may prove what is that good and acceptable and perfect will of God." Becoming disciplined means developing mental resolve—the guts and stamina to train yourself to work out your challenges and problems before plunging into a relationship or hopping from one relationship to another.

We often run from discipline because it's not easy. Hebrews 12:11 says, "No discipline seems pleasant at the time, but painful. Later on, however, it produces a harvest of righteousness and peace for those who have been trained by it" (NIV). Discipline takes training and *is* painful, but the results are too good to miss! This means that first I have to make up my mind that I am going to be disciplined.

Important in developing a disciplined life is recognizing and facing our weaknesses and spending time alone to receive God's council. In whatever aspect of your life discipline is required, seek God's help. If this means avoiding certain places and people, commit to that decision and use God's Word to nurture you when you are tempted.

Seek out Christian friends. Psalm 1:1 says, "Blessed is the man / Who walks not in the counsel of the ungodly, / Nor stands in the path of sinners, / Nor sits in the seat of the scornful." I have to be careful where I go because I can't go everywhere and still be God's reflection. Being disciplined does not happen just because we want discipline. We have to work for it. But that's when the devil will start messing with your mind. Discipline means: I know myself, my weakness and my strengths. Everyone has both. After I make up my mind—make a sincere resolution to change—I then ask if this atmosphere is physically and spiritually healthy for me. If you have a problem discerning what is healthy for you, use the power of God to stand strong against temptations. If that does not work, find other Christians who are like who you want to be.

To secure a disciplined life, maintain a righteous regime. You need a system or plan in place for your consistent spiritual nourishment. When you plan your day or downtime, include time in the Word. Make an effort to nurture your soul like you nurture your body. You don't even have to have an agenda, just show up. Open your Bible. God will surprise you with a rich message you could never have foreseen. We have no problem making plans for the football game or movie, so plan time getting closer to God. God will be delighted and He is faithful to His promises as well. You are in for blessings when you meditate on the Word of God.

6. TRAVEL TO NEW PLACES

One of the most enriching ways to inform our spiritual connection with God and with self happens when we intentionally place ourselves in unfamiliar cultures and situations. It is no understatement that you learn about yourself when you travel. Any kind of travel—meaning to another country or at least spending time in another culture—will bring a wealth of inward knowledge. Ezekiel 40 gives an example of spiritual travel where a vision transports the prophet Ezekiel to a physical location—the land of Israel. And the point of the travel seems to be information gathering. God urges the traveler to watch and listen so that he can return and tell others who won't get to travel what he has seen and heard.

Adding a service or mission component to travel makes the experience even richer. Travel that transforms comes in many opportunities. Few experiences are more informing personally than a short-term mission trip. Learning to respect other languages, heritage, scenery, and customs in God's expansive world can enhance the perspective of one who is journeying toward wholeness.

> **Travel can transform and groom you for wholeness.**

Transformational travel has everything to do with being aware of our tendencies toward a superiority complex. When we only know about our society, we tend to think we've got it all together and ignore the fact that we could learn from others. Travel, even if it is only across town or to an unfamiliar neighborhood, allows us to see the world from a different angle and find renewed humility, genuine concern, and love for people who are different.

7. PURSUE GOD'S PURPOSE FOR YOUR LIFE

Jeremiah 29:11 says that God has a plan of peace for us, not one of evil, and He wants to give that good gift to you.

Always remember that you have to be after God's purpose for your life, not somebody else's preplanned purpose for you. Know who you are and what God wants for you to do. Then you will have a clear vision of the way ahead if someone throws an obstacle in your path or tries to circumvent your journey.

Before connecting with someone, develop yourself as a healthy individual. Align your purpose with God. Then get education and training. Don't talk about it to a lot of people until you talk to God and ask for guidance and the resources you need to carry out God's purpose for you.

Be ready for challenges as well. If you've applied for college or a special school and you aren't accepted, don't let that stump you. Recognize that there's more than one path to take. Ask, what's the next plan? Aggressively pursue your dreams! Don't waste your time waiting on someone else. Make another plan and act on it. Part of pursuing God's purpose for you is that when you come to a relationship, you have something to offer—you bring something to the table. Sure, you love him or her, but what do you bring to the relationship?

Beware, however, because people will be intimidated by your success. Some of that is natural, because your interests and new experiences are different or more specific; you are moving and working in different places. Your movement highlights their lack of movement. You aren't visiting the same places or doing the things you did before you began your journey toward

> **Expect your growth to intimidate and eliminate.**

wholeness. That creates a physical and emotional distance that your friends might not adjust to without difficulty.

8. BE COMPLETE IN CHRIST

The last step in becoming relationship ready and preparing yourself as a whole individual leads to becoming complete in Christ, the head of all principality and power. Just as you call and text your friends and family, keep regular daily contact with Jesus. Being complete in Christ implies that in all areas of your life—relationships, family and friends, spiritual commitments, occupations, finances, recreation and sports, travel, and so on—you are confident in who you are in God.

Paul says in Philippians 4:11, "I have learned in whatever state I am, to be content." Walk confidently in Him, rooted, built up, established in the faith. When I have a healthy, active relationship with Jesus Christ, I am complete in Him and He's enough for me. Completion in Christ shows a leap toward maturity. You've learned how to be hungry and full, how to abase and abound, how to adjust to circumstances. We can do all things through Christ who strengthens us. We can do it because we're in a relationship with Christ.

Now you are ready for a holy hookup.

THINK ABOUT THIS

1. What lessons have you learned from your past relationships? How have you used pain to help you grow?

2. What is the danger in trying to be the savior of a relationship?

3. Where would you like to travel and learn new things?

4. Your response to these questions will help you judge if you are in a wholesome relationship:

> Is my love for God growing?
>
> Do I read the Bible daily?
>
> Do I pray regularly?
>
> Do I obey the voice of God?
>
> Is my commitment to God and to godly things increasing or decreasing?

5. How ready are you to get into a relationship? And if you are already in a relationship, how ready are you to work on it to align it with God's purposes?

MEN: MEET THE STANDARD

In the beginning, God said it was not good for the man to be alone. Every man was created to be in a loving relationship. How does anyone find love? Too often people kiss frogs to find their soul mate, because real love is elusive and many people don't understand what it really is, what it looks or feels like.

WHAT WOMEN SAY ABOUT MEN WHO MEET THE STANDARD

Women, understand this: men are different. We have our own set of issues. Men are not as inclined to be as emotional as women are. When we were young, we were told not to cry and not be punks. We associate being in touch with our emotions with being soft, unmanly. It's important for you to understand that we prefer approaching relationships not from our emotions but from our heads. Men are not socially acclimated the way women are. Your relationship radar is sharper; your personal connections are quicker. Your desire for commitment and permanency in relationship happens much earlier than it does for a guy. This is no accident; there are significant reasons for those differing patterns.

1. HE IS SAVED, A MAN OF FAITH

A woman cannot properly be covered unless she has a man in her life who is covered by God. "Properly covered" means she is guided by God's authority and her husband's authority. I'm not talking about any woman—I mean a godly woman. She needs to also feel that her husband will cover her. You remember Joseph and Mary, when Mary was pregnant by the Holy Ghost. If anybody deserved to have a real issue with this, it is Joseph. Think about it:

Your woman: I'm pregnant.
You: By who?
Your woman: The Holy Ghost!
You (scratching your head): All right, Holy Ghost. . . . Hmm.

Instead, Joseph shows us that once the Holy Spirit revealed to him what took place within his wife, he covered her and took her to another place. As a godly man, you have to be sensitive to the Holy Spirit and the emotional things that take place within your woman. Because it's important to understand he did not set her out, he covered her, and that's all about support, because at the end of the day that woman's going to cover you.

As a man I want to be so full of the Word that I respond with my faith. When I'm stormed by unexpected trauma or circumstances, I am not shaken. In fact, during those challenging times my faith is strengthened because I know God is in control. Although I am an adult, I can access that child-like faith that waits for God's intervention. Women need men who can operate like that and see faith manifested in their relationships.

Faithful to God, faithful to the church, faithful—he's a man who you don't have to drag to church. He's a man who says, "As for me and my house, we're going. I'm faithful to what God called me to do, I'm faithful." If you are in relationship with a man who values friendship, look at his friends. Remember the psalm: "Blessed is the man / Who walks not in the counsel of the ungodly, / Nor stands in the path of sinners, / Nor sits in the seat of the scornful" (Psalm 1:1)—the man who has the right friendships. This man delights himself in the law of the Lord; he has faith because he's in the Word. Then he is faithful, because he acts out based on what he knows.

2. HE IS COMPASSIONATE AND KNOWS HOW TO BE A FRIEND

A compassionate man identifies with someone else's needs. Out of that identification, the compassionate man responds by doing for others as he wants done to himself. It's hard for a woman to resist a compassionate man. Especially when those feelings are natural and she isn't expecting that response. He naturally responds to the need because of how it touches his spirit. Compassion is the cure for selfishness and has energy for giving.

By the same token, friendliness cannot be scripted. Good friendships usually bless relationships because a good friendship is good for one's soul. And that goodness spreads. Just as you can judge a woman by her friends, she can judge you by yours. When she sees how you honor friendships, it speaks to your character.

Be agreeable, be sympathetic, be loving, be compassion-ate, be humble. That goes for anyone, no exceptions. No re-taliation. No sharp-tongued sarcasm. Instead, bless—that's your job, to bless. You'll be a blessing and receive a blessing.

3. HE UNDERSTANDS AND VALUES FIDELITY

For many women fidelity is a must and if a man lacks it, the deal is over. Women don't want a man who cheats. The goal is that this man is committed to God and studies God's Word. When he loves God's commandments, there's too much Word in him to tip out on her. He understands what fidelity means, so when he takes a vow, he means it.

Surprisingly, most single people today don't really believe that fidelity is a realistic expectation. Sadly, many women go into relationships thinking that it's not a question of whether the man will cheat, but when. They know the messages our uncles gave us: "How many girlfriends you got, boy? You only got one?"

Women have seen forty-year marriages end in adultery. They've seen powerful—even honorable—men make stupid choices over another woman. It leaves them feeling that all men will do it at some point in their lives.

A woman wants her man to say, "Baby, I want you. You are enough." Most marriages begin with young people and usually the man is sexually on fire. The woman may be won-dering if he'll still be on fire ten years from now. A married woman needs to know that she's enough, that she alone satisfies and pleases her husband. Likewise, a single woman needs to know that she's enough—that she's attractive enough, that she has all the things you need, and that when you're in the mall, you're not still trying to check out other women looking for something better.

A woman will say, "You can have all this stuff, the house, the benefits; I just want a man who has integrity." That other stuff helps, but at the end of the day a woman wants a man who is telling the truth.

Men, we have a long way to go to prove to them that we value fidelity. If you are in a relationship and haven't felt like fidelity was that important, do not keep it to yourself. The two of you need to talk and figure out a way to work on this.

4. HE IS SINCERE, SENSITIVE, AND UNDERSTANDING

This is the monster that most men struggle with. This requires that you understand her feelings and past experiences. Reading that may send chills up a man's spine. But men, most of her pain can be traced to dysfunctional relationships with other men: father, uncle, brother, or former boyfriend.

Words don't have the same impact on men as they do on women. Back in the day I was pledging in this certain fraternity; and that's when hazing was not really legal, but they did it anyway. The frat brothers could say all kinds of stuff to me and it wouldn't bother me; but when they physically applied pain, that would grab my undivided attention. Then you know we had some line sisters pledging sorority. And they would be crying. We would ask what was wrong and they would let go of this litany of phrases that the sorority sisters said to them. It hurt them badly. They'd cry, "They're saying this about me." Their sorority wouldn't have to inflict any physical pain; all they had to do was just say something mean—"Let me break you down, Sister Soldier," or words to that effect.

Every man needs to know that words are so powerful to a woman. In counseling I often hear the man say, "I didn't ever hit her!" He doesn't understand that he hit her with his mouth! To her, his verbal attacks were just as painful as a physical attack. Words have the same impact on her. But most men don't see words as violence. Women view words as violence. I have to raise this question: In the Garden of Eden, why did the serpent go to the woman? Because she was more susceptible. He knew that his words would have more impact on her.

Men have to understand that women aren't stupid. They know when we're being sincere and when we try to fool them. They may sit up and let us tell that lie and keep telling that lie; and they'll say, "Umm hmm, all right." But they are not stupid, they know! Romans 12:17 cautions, "Recompense to no man evil for evil. Provide things [that are] honest" (KJV). Women want honesty in relationships. They appreciate it and usually reward it with understanding and cooperation. If you've messed up, just swallow your pride and say you messed up and ask them to help you work through the issue.

There's a saying: It's one thing to call me a fool, but it's another thing to make me think I'm a fool. When you are dishonest, it not only dishonors you, it dishonors the other person as well. Romans 13:13 says, "Let us walk honestly, as in the day; not in rioting and drunkenness, not in chambering and wantonness, not in strife and envying" (KJV). In other words, just be honest. If there is one thing you ought to be able to do, it is to be honest with the people you say you love.

5. HE'S A MAN WHO VALUES FAMILY

Most women know to check out the way a man interacts with his natural family before marrying him. It usually gives a clear indication of the kind of family man he will be. They know to look at how his father treats his mother and how he treats his mother. They study how he interacts with his family. He has to value people and have a healthy relationship with family. It's important that his love is clear and that he enjoys being around them. However, because we live in a dysfunctional society, many men and women do not have healthy relationships with their parents. If they have found parental substitutes, an aunt or uncle or some older persons they connect with on a familial basis, those relationships may have helped them understand and appreciate family. If that is not the case, it is important to discuss how not having a healthy family has affected a person's personality and behavior.

It's also important to see how the man interacts with children. If a woman wants children and the man doesn't, that may be a signal to change the relationship. But even if you both do want children, that is a subject that requires long and deep discussions.

6. HE KNOWS HOW TO BE THE FATHER

A man who is a father is to provide for, love, teach, and chasten his children. First Timothy 5:8 urges that, "If anyone does not provide for his relatives, and especially for his immediate family, he has denied the faith and is worse than an unbeliever" (NIV). He has to see that his children develop in all areas just as Jesus developed in wisdom, stature, and favor with men and God (Luke 2:52).

A father's goal is that his children mature: "bring them up in the training and admonition of the Lord" (Ephesians 6:4). If he does not provide for them, he provokes them to wrath, he makes them angry. When you see some young man or young woman who is rebelling and who has these issues, it's a good guess they are from families where daddy did not provide for them. They are simply responding to the plight of having to grow up too soon.

With all that our society has learned and with all the Bible teaches, we know that children must have a solid foundation. "Train up a child in the way he should go, and when he is old he will not depart" (Proverbs 22:6). So the man who would be a father must ask, "Am I prepared to be that kind of father?"

We cannot ignore or forget—as the scripture says: "And you have forgotten the exhortation which speaks to you as to sons: / 'My son, do not despise the chastening of the LORD, / Nor be discouraged when you are rebuked by Him; / For whom the LORD loves He chastens, / And scourges every son whom He receives'" (Hebrews 12:5-6). "Chasten" means to whip, correct, whoop, whatever you call it. The key is that you not strike out or punish in anger. If you are angry, wait and talk calmly with your child. That in itself takes discipline and it's a good way to model discipline for your child. And undoubtedly there are instances when an immediate punishment is demanded. But the correction is something that should not be ignored, because it shows your love for the child. The reason the Lord whoops you is because He loves you.

7. HE IS FOCUSED

The man God has prepared to pursue the godly woman cannot be easily distracted by circumstances. He's focused, knowing where God is taking him. He has a plan and it's not just pipe dreams. He's not just sitting around fittin' to do something; he's not sitting around saying, "Well, I'm working on something." It's not just his freestyling thoughts. He got a plan for life that he has carried to God and petitioned God for guidance on. His plan is written and he's clear about his goals; so clear that he has crafted a financial plan to help that happen. If you ask him about it, he can tell it. However, he is protective of it, knowing that talking a lot about it steals the energy necessary to make it happen.

Along with focus is motivation. Women want a man who is financially secure or at least has a plan to be; because that is an indication that he is capable of supporting her. Laziness and lack of ambition with no plans for moving forward are not traits that make a good husband. She doesn't want a wimp, pushover, or someone who gives up easily. She needs someone who strives for things to happen, not waits for things to happen.

8. HE VALUES COMMUNICATION

Lack of communication is usually at the crux of relationship conflicts. Many men struggle with communicating at the level that women require. Women want us to express our emotions, and that is difficult for most men. When we do participate, though, usually we are pleased with the results. It is not something most men delve into easily. But it's crucial for men to realize how important communication is to a woman. Because of that, men try to walk that path.

An essential part of successful communication is asking questions. Many times people share information with one another and the response is something that stops the conversation cold, like, "Oh, really?" The person says yes and it ends there. The key to thinking of follow-up questions is to look at her and listen. Give her your undivided attention. Listen to the feelings underneath what she is saying. Look at her body language. This is huge when hearing your wife's stories for getting the full impact of what she's trying to tell you. Your participation gives you a perspective into what she is experiencing. Your questions reflect your perspective and her answers give you her perspective. That helps her know how you are processing the information she's giving.

"Death and life are in the power of the tongue, / And those who love it will eat its fruit" (Proverbs 18:21). A woman needs to know how you are feeling and what you think about an issue. She needs to know that you've given some thought to whatever the topic is, and she values your opinion. It's interesting that the following verse compliments the wife: "He who finds a wife finds a good thing, / And obtains favor from the LORD" (v. 22). It seems to suggest that if you can't talk to her, you sure can't love her.

What good is it to find her if you have nothing to say to her? Because when she shows up, you've got to have something to say. When Eve showed up, Adam had something to say: "Oh woman, I see all inside of you! You are bone of my bone, flesh of my flesh." His smart statement implies he had been checking out her interior before commenting on her exterior. He was having a deep conversation that he initiated. When she showed up, Adam initiated the conversation. Women need a man who can hold a conversation and not just hold the phone.

9. HE KNOWS HOW TO HANDLE HIS FINANCES

Financial accountability is prime, not only in a relationship, but in planning your future. The more experience you have with money, the more you respect it and its power. Women say the man doesn't have to be rich, but be reasonable about spending and manage your debt. If you're not sure of your financial behavior, ask these questions: How do you handle your money? Do you pay your bills on time? Do you know what compound interest on a loan means? Do you have a 401K? Do you know what an IRA is? Do you tithe? How do you manage the money God has given? Do you understand savings and checking accounts? Do you live out of your front pocket and walk around like you're a baller because you have $500 in your front left pocket, or do you have money in the bank? Do you own real estate? Do you understand appreciable and depreciable assets?

These are the kinds of things we men have to work on. If you're planning on spending a future with a woman, you have to be able to hold it down financially. How can she submit to someone who can't even consistently pay the rent? In addition, a good man leaves an inheritance to his children's children. This means you've made decisions and plans on how to grow the money and assets you have. It has nothing to do with how much money you make, it's how you manage the money God has given to you.

10. HE'S A MAN WHO KNOWS HOW TO HAVE FUN

He may be focused and hard-working, but it doesn't mean he's boring or a recluse. Most men like to get out and do stuff. Women want somebody to have fun with. Men, we got to learn how to have fun, to step out of the familiar and not take ourselves too seriously. Travel and putting yourself in different surroundings helps you move from the sometimes-too-serious mode and the grind of day-to-day living. Take an interest in new things and give your partner an opportunity to interact in different settings. When you look back over two months and see that you've not done any fun activity, take that as a warning! Get out and have some fun!

11. HE VALUES FITNESS

Women want active, healthy men; and sometimes they need the man to help move them into making healthier choices. This is another area where the church is silent. Take the lead in your relationship. When you see that you can't walk up the stairs without wheezing or find yourself going out of your way to avoid extra steps, that's a sign that you are neglecting your body. A godly man cannot neglect his temple. Adopting an active lifestyle will not only benefit your body but is also a great example to your children. If you don't have children, use the time that you exercise to mentor a youth.

Men and women have to develop higher standards about what we put into our bodies. We need to change our mind-sets about the fast-food option and be more insistent about regular exercise and healthy eating. We can't complain that we don't feel well, when the problem has to do with lack of exercise and improper eating. Making healthy choices for our bodies is another way we can honor God. When we make healthy changes, we extend our time for serving God and for being with the people we love. We want our children to have both parents for as long as God blesses us. But as with anything, if we abuse what God has given us, we will surely lose it.

12. HE IS A MAN WITH VISION

A woman needs a man who has a plan for life. Too often women want to know what a man is working on, what are his dreams and aspirations. As the scripture says, "Write the vision and make it plain . . . that he who reads it may run with it" (Habakkuk 2:2, paraphrased). Understand this is about vision: you don't need to have arrived, but at least to be on your way there. Vision will always raise you out of your present situation and it is always progressively revealed.

My imagination needs the stimulation that comes from association with successful people. A man with vision is part of God's plan to rescue him out of his current situation. So when a man is a dreamer, it may intimidate others because his dream sheds light on their inability to deal with their current situation. But when a man has a vision, he's able to move beyond stagnation, excuses, and limitations. In other words, he won't be sitting around making excuses and blaming the system. That man, because of his belief in God's desires for him, expects to see God doing great things in his life. That's who the godly woman is looking for, not a man sitting back and making excuses as to why he can't do this and why he can't do that or blaming his circumstances. She needs a man who has vision.

When God spoke to Abraham, he got a vision, but Sarah was needed to complete that vision. It's important to get this. When a man shares his vision, a woman will ask, "Are you willing to pay the price for your vision?" Any man who is willing to pay the price for his vision is a man willing to work to make that vision a reality, whether it means getting an education, saving money, or doing the work it takes to make it happen, all while asking for God's guidance. He is committed to doing better and to enduring whatever it takes to bring the vision to fruition. He shares this vision with his wife and can articulate clearly how that woman fits in his vision. He knows she will do her part to help the vision. Women need men who have vision, who see beyond their reality.

13. HE IS COMMITTED AND HAS CONVICTION

Unfortunately, commitment is something that most men fear. So any man who is committed is a man who has a right to expect something of the Lord. Because of that, any woman of God is looking for a man who has commitment. If he's not committed to anything, she will expect nothing from him.

In Psalm 1, the Bible talks about the commitment of a man whose delight is in the Lord's law, on which he meditates night and day. He's a committed man of God who day and night enjoys being with God. The woman does not have to beg him to come to church or to pray; she doesn't have to coax him to be spiritual, because God's Word excites him and he gets a kick out of learning the teachings of God.

As Christ gave Himself for the church, the man must then be willing to give himself for the relationship. So the woman of God is saying, "I know how much you love *you*, but I need to know that you love *me*." This man has convictions and knows why he believes in them. His convictions are not born out of blind faith or without contemplation. His lifestyle backs up his beliefs.

14. HE IS CONNECTED TO HER AND KNOWS HOW TO CELEBRATE HER

Many times we hear people say, "He gets me" or "She knows where I'm coming from." They mean that with this person they don't have to spend a lot of time explaining their point of view or their thinking. When others may misunderstand, this person is on the same page with them. This makes the person feel like they are not alone. Misunderstandings put distance between two people, and too many misunderstandings are a sign that the two may not be connecting on a number of levels.

Being understood by your mate is huge. Just as misunderstandings bring distance, understanding strengthens the connection between two people. This connection is powerful and invisible. When we see two people that we think physically don't fit, there's probably a strong and powerful connection they enjoy. It's priceless.

When a man is connected to his woman, he also knows her strengths and weaknesses, and he knows her heart. When she accomplishes something, he is genuinely interested. He watches her progress and celebrates her victories. There is nothing so bitter as completing a vigorous task or overcoming a challenge and your mate not noticing. When that happens, an invisible distance surfaces that separates her from him. The victorious person feels empty because the one person they'd like to celebrate with doesn't know the story. The key to avoiding that is—guess what?—intentional communication and active listening.

Knowing how to celebrate her helps you participate in her story. Many times a man is intimidated by a woman's success because her accomplishments may seem to highlight his deficiencies. But men and women should take this as an opportunity to emphasize the oneness between the two. Just as when you bleed, she hurts, when she succeeds, you feel that is your success too. Just as you are connected to her pain, you are part of her achievements and vice versa. Just as you need her support when you do well, she needs yours. She needs to feel that you are proud of her and her accomplishments. If she receives a promotion at work, make a big deal of it—celebrate her and celebrate your lives together. Your attitude is to celebrate no matter how minor the accomplishment, because it's major to you because your baby did it. Just as giving brings you more blessings than the receiver, learning to celebrate your woman brings the celebration right back to you!

THINK ABOUT THIS

1. Which standards can you easily meet? Which standards do you need to address?

2. What advice would you give to a man or woman to help that person sustain a godly relationship?

3. If you were talking to a young person about a man's role, what would you say?

WOMEN: MEET THE STANDARD

In the movie *The Preacher's Wife*, Whitney Houston's character, Julia, and the Reverend Henry Biggs (Courtney Vance) have a refreshingly solid relationship. However, because of the demands of the church, his schedule has kept him from spending time with her and their son. During that time Julia is smitten by the attention she receives from the angel Dudley, played by Denzel Washington. Her mother, who believes in the strong foundation of Julia's and Henry's marriage, takes a proactive (although typical mother-in-law) step by initiating a conversation with Dudley. She invites him to take a walk with her and tells him in no uncertain terms that he needs to go help some other church and that if he doesn't leave, she will conveniently develop an illness that requires her to stay longer so that she can block any advances he might make. Dudley tries to assure her that she is wrong. (Dudley is actually sent by God to help Reverend Biggs.) But she knows and the audience knows the danger of a good-looking man getting too close to any wife—no matter how strong the marital foundation.

Women are uniquely made. God gave women two gifts at a level that men don't have—strength and wisdom. God gave not brute strength, but internal strength. Women have the propensity to handle pain—emotional and physical—better than men. God also gave women incredible wisdom. Women grasp wisdom more quickly than men. In the book of Genesis, God would not release the woman until the man was ready for her. She was inside of Adam, but God did not make her, build her, rib upon rib, until the man had his stuff together. She is a woman of strength and a woman of wisdom; and even if she's not there yet, you can trust that she's got ability. She just needs to know and access those gifts.

God is at work positioning women and men for relationships. According to the Bible, the man is prepared first by God, given the tools and intellect to pursue the good woman that God will position for him. As God creates the woman, she too, is prepared for the man. God gives her status, intellect, attitude, personality, wisdom, emotional footing, too many attributes to list; but these attributes position her to participate in this grand familial plan. "He who finds a wife finds a good thing, / And obtains favor from the LORD" (Proverbs 18:22).

THE GOOD WOMAN EQUALS FAVOR FROM GOD

Proverbs 31 gives the biblical standard for who a wife should be. To pattern herself by and wrap herself in these virtues will help her become a good wife, a healthy woman in terms of God's perspective. And it will give the husband a home established in peace. The message of Proverbs 31 is presented via the voice of a mother offering powerful wisdom to her son about the outstanding woman she—no doubt—wants for him and his family. The description begins in verse 10 with the question: "Who can find a virtuous [woman]?" Where is she? She is rare, valuable, unique; not easily found. It takes great care and attention to find her. When a man finds this kind of woman, it's like he's hit the jackpot; he's found a treasure.

Verses 11, 12, and 23 speak of the relationship between husband and wife. He trusts her without hesitation and never regrets that trust. She deliberately does things to validate his confidence. The text talks about her as an asset, not a liability; she brings value to their relationship—things that money cannot buy. She is not a ball and chain around the man's leg. Rather, she enables her man to live a freer, more generous life. She is never spiteful and treats him generously. If she ever finds herself in a position where she would harm the man, it's time for her to step away.

Verses 15, 17, and 18 speak of her work ethic. She's up before dawn preparing breakfast for her family, organizing the day. She is domestically skilled. That she enjoys her work is evident, because she's eager to get started. She's not afraid of hard work. She rolls up her sleeves and values the worth of her work. One version (*The Message*) says she "is in no hurry to call it quits for the day."

She is concerned that her household is well and nutritiously fed. She studies good nutrition because she wants her children to be healthy. She understands the difference between fixing something to eat and cooking. When you throw something in the microwave and it's ready in two minutes, you're just fixing something to eat. Real meal preparation takes time. And men, you may have to help her with the kids and chores to give her the time she needs. Meal planning is important and challenging.

Eight verses in this 21-verse salute to the virtuous woman relate to her financial intelligence and business acumen: shopping, trading, and real estate purchases. No gripes from women on that, right? She is skilled at sewing, knitting, and designing clothing. She knows when her family looks good. She dresses appropriately; she is modest, yet in style, and carries herself with dignity. And she dresses her children that way. She's excellent at making crafts for her home. This woman is a predecessor of B. Smith and Martha Stewart. This virtuous woman possesses confidence in navigating contracts, evaluating, and conducting successful transactions. Remember, men, she was whole before she met you. She came to the party with some cheese. This kind of woman doesn't sit around waiting on some man to do it all for her. But she does need you to value and respect her accomplishments.

Verse 27 explains that she knows her family well, giving consistent attention to their educational and emotional needs. Her family is not idle or bored because she challenges their skills and intellect by keeping them busy and productive. This includes everyone in the house. She is a wise woman of hope, not afraid of tomorrow, but facing the future with a smile. She is clever and sharp and knows how to encourage those who are suffering. She gives worthy knowledge and kind words to those God sends her way.

When it's time to speak for the house, she lets her husband do it; she doesn't compete with her husband in the city gates. One of the most embarrassing things a woman can do to a man is try to compete with him in public. His speaking for the family doesn't devalue her, because he respects and values her opinions. He leans on her for advice, because her deeds reveal that she is spiritual and connected to God. She is quick to help anyone in need and reaches out to the poor. This is a strong example to her children, who respect and bless her.

The chapter ends with her husband praising her. According to him she outclasses all women because of the wonderful things she has done. Many women are charming and beautiful, but this God-fearing woman is admired and praised.

WHAT MEN SAY ABOUT WOMEN WHO MEET THE STANDARD

These characteristics are gleaned from conversations and interviews with men who answered the question: "What do you want/need from a woman?" So you will hear their voices in this list. Their responses were measured against God's words and are offered with fervent prayer that they will bless you, the woman who seeks to meet God's standard.

1. SHE LOVES AND IS ANCHORED IN GOD

This is a spiritually grounded, praying woman. She is a woman who loves God, who's no stranger in church. She is in a committed relationship with God, values and pursues spiritual growth, and enjoys worshiping and sharing in the Word of the Lord.

The woman knows how to pray. Often men don't mature as quickly as women. We have our issues; we make stupid mistakes and do stupid stuff. Many of us are still working out our relationship with God. We need women who know how to pray prayers that target our specific weaknesses and needs. Men need that ministry of prayer, so we need women who love to do God's will and who are praying wives. When you are connected to what God is doing in our lives, you understand these kinds of things. So when God gives us vision and responsibilities in the home, we come together and pray about it.

This woman is a sharp contrast to one who is merely psycho-spiritual. "Psycho-spiritual" defines people who are so enamored and consumed with theological words and terminology that they lose themselves and using this terminology becomes their spirituality. It's difficult for the psycho-spiritual person to have a normal conversation. And you cannot have a real, meaningful relationship with them. You say, "Hello, how are you?" The psycho-spiritual person goes into a theological performance and responds, "Praise God. You know the Lord is telling me to tell you something. Hallelujah. You need to hear this message from the Lord." This is all the time. When you can't have a normal conversation without saying, "You know the Lord was saying this to me . . ." we will probably have some communication issues. Many are afraid of psycho-spiritual people, because there is no space or balance in their world.

The anchored woman walks with God and uses spirituality in her day-to-day life. If she's confronted with adversity, she doesn't despair. Her faith is strengthened in adversity because she knows God is about to do something. If her job is phased out, she can smile, because she knows she has given her employer her best and she simply says, "God is in control of this thing." Her co-workers don't understand her, because they are not familiar with someone who demonstrates the peace that passes understanding. She conducts her life in a Christ-like way. She knows that when a door closes, God provides a window for something even more promising than her previous experiences.

2. SHE PROVIDES HONEST, TIMELY, LOVING COMMUNICATION

"[Speak] the truth in love" that you "may grow up in all things into Him who is the head—Christ" (Ephesians 4:15). Women have to know how and when to talk to men. Women, when your man comes home, you have to tune in to his spirit; check his posture and listen to his tone to know whether it's a good time to bring up whatever's on your mind. You have to strategize when to share truth with him.

Often, because many men are not natural communicators, we are defensive about entering into a deep conversation. So when you say, "I've got to talk to you about something," our minds immediately go on the defensive. Inwardly we're asking, "What? What did I do? What?" We assume something's wrong. There may be nothing wrong and we know that; but you have to know that's how we process that statement.

Timing—you have to know how and when to talk to us. Here's a tip: when you hear the theme music from ESPN's Sports Center, be clear—this is not the time to talk to us, because we are zoned out. Even if you ask us to turn it off, you set us up for unfocused conversation. Don't make us compete with other things that have value and recognize that we value things that you think are frivolous and vice versa. All of us want communication that exemplifies godliness, but timing is always an issue.

It's important to figure out when is the best time and space to talk about an issue. "A fool uttereth all his mind: but a wise man keepeth it in till afterwards" (Proverbs 29:11 KJV). A foolish person will tell you everything on his or her mind without gauging whether it's the appropriate time to speak it. A wise person will say, "Now I got some stuff on my mind, but I'm going to wait until I have his undivided attention." Offer him the respect you give any person whose full attention you desire.

When you communicate with men, take care that you are loving, honest, and concise. Men want to know exactly what you want. James 5:12 says to let your yes be yes and let your no be no. Often we don't multitask as women do, so when we ask you questions, if you say yes to something today and then no on Wednesday or Thursday, it's confusing. We want yes to be yes, so we don't have to juggle all that and wonder if you really meant it the last time you said no. This also includes being up-front and not trying to manipulate the relationship. If you are a man reading this, I know you are smiling. Men don't want to feel they have to be mind-readers or have to interpret signals just to receive a true communication from women. They don't

> **Resist manipulating the relationship to fit your expectations.**

want to feel there's an unspoken undercurrent of deception going on.

Men do not appreciate being forced to move faster in relationships than they're ready to move. Most times, when men begin relationships, they don't move as fast as women. We're not acclimated or programmed for relationships like women are. Remember, most girls had dolls and played house growing up. Boys had action figures and played war games. So for at least fifteen years before they start seriously dating, most women have been accustomed to seeing themselves in the home/family scenario. For that same amount of time, men have become comfortable with fighting and sports games.

When a man goes on that first lunch or dinner with a woman, recognize that most women have fast-forwarded the relationship and the altar is already in sight. After that first date, some women stop by the store to pick up a bride's magazine; they text their friends: "Girl, he's the right size and height. What colors should I go for?" He's thinking, "That was a nice lunch." So listen, women: men don't want to be manipulated into relationships before they're ready. That should make sense to you, because you know how unsuccessful premature relationships can be.

3. SHE IS GENEROUS WITH ENCOURAGING WORDS

"Baby, you can do this. Keep your fists up; they're trying to sneak up on you over there." After he's weathered a storm at work, he doesn't want to come home and fight with you; his war is over. He needs to know that when he comes home, he's coming for reinforcement—not more battles. His home

71

ought to be a retreat, where he gets encouragement, where he gets built up, where he gets affirmation.

"Above all things have fervent charity among yourselves: for charity shall cover the multitude of sins" (1 Peter 4:8 KJV). When you love me and communicate that love to me, it covers a multitude of sins. A woman is comfortable with honest, loving, timely communication because she wants that for herself.

4. SHE HAS THE RIGHT ATTITUDE

A continual dripping on a very rainy day
  And a contentious woman are alike. (Proverbs 27:15)

Better to dwell in the wilderness,
  Than with a contentious and angry woman.
  (Proverbs 21:19)

These words can be used to describe a woman with a bad attitude. A man would rather live in the wilderness than to come home to your cantankerous self. Sometimes that negative attitude pops up when we just try to speak. Some women just seem to have a built-in nasty button. Here is an example:

Man: How are you?
Attitude woman (grunts): Fine!
Man: How are you, Beautiful?
Attitude woman (spoken angrily): Who you talking to?

Women, please understand: just because he's complimenting you or speaking to you does not mean he's trying to holler at you or he has ulterior motives. He's being a Christian gentleman. It's okay to smile and simply receive the compliment, whether you agree with it or not. It's okay to be a gracious woman without being flirtatious. If something is going on in your life that makes you argumentative or affects your attitude, take care of that. Seek out a Christian counselor, read the Scriptures, and ask for God's guidance for strength to overcome the problem. The spirit of Christ can't dwell in a contentious person. You want to attract people, not drive them off with a negative spirit.

5. SHE IS AUTHENTIC

Men are looking for something real; they are tired of meeting your representative, the person you want them to think you are. Just be you, because when you're married and you roll over in the morning, he *will see* the real you. Just keep it real and be who you are. You don't have to front. Be content with how God made you. This doesn't mean you can't put your best foot forward and that you shouldn't try to make improvements. We want you to be familiar with beauty products and to take care of your body. We are all striving for perfection, but remain true to yourself.

There comes a point when you say, "Look, this is who I am, take it or leave it. I'm not going to try to mold myself to be what somebody wants me to be. I'm working on who God wants me to be, but this is who I am." Be authentic, the real thing, no additives, no preservatives.

6. SHE ADAPTS TO A VARIETY OF SITUATIONS

She is a woman who goes to a business luncheon, then to a formal affair, and then comes home and is wife and mother; she is gracious and generous and is as comfortable with *people* on the margins of society as she is with the wealthy. She adapts quickly to her roles, because the people she deals with in all situations are important to her.

Sometimes I call some of my bishop friends on the phone. So I call one of these guys and the wife answers the phone. After greeting her I say, "May I speak to So-and-So?" And I hear some of them call to him, saying, "Bishop, telephone." I'm shocked, thinking, *You actually call him Bishop at home?* My feeling is, that won't work in my house. No! I'm not Bishop Walker at home. And don't call me Pastor at home. No. We get new names at home, because in my home there's going to be some stuff going on where Bishop won't fit. My wife knows that too.

7. SHE UNDERSTANDS WHAT SUBMISSION REALLY IS

We need women who are connected in the spirit, but we also need women who understand submission. *I know. I said it.* Godly men are not drawn to women of the world; they are drawn to women who have godly desires. That word *submission* expresses being subordinate, or adapting to God's will; it means to follow, to humbly be in obedience to someone else's will rather than your own. In Ephesians 5:22, the Bible says, "Wives, submit yourselves unto your own husbands" (KJV).

Understand that submission is really co-mission. *The wife is supposed to submit to that man as he is submitted to God.* She cannot submit to a man if he isn't submitted to God. But if he is submitted to God, it is a joy for her to be co-submitted with him because they

> **Submission is really co-mission.**

are both under God and they have the order of God where she is under him. This is a covering, a protection that she receives under God's provision. She needs that covering. Are you seeing what I'm saying now? Being a strong sister is beneficial and wonderful; but at the end of the day, you need to be a godly woman, covered by and submitted to God and your husband.

8. SHE VALUES ACADEMICS

This woman values the intellect. She doesn't necessarily have to have a college degree, but she should be always seeking to improve her education. When a woman has academic training, it's clear that she has a strong desire for success—for herself, her children, her husband, and her church and community.

This ambition is a significant value for families. Your potential husband will want to blend his life with someone who is trying to achieve something, not somebody sitting around waiting on the gravy train to come. Your dreams and visions will attract someone who also has dreams and visions that will enhance the kingdom of God.

As a woman, what are you bringing to the table? What is God showing you? How can your gifts and goals support or blend with your partner's? People may not associate the word *merger* with marriage, but in a real sense that's what happens. Your wholeness merges with his; your assets merge with his.

9. SHE IS SELF-SUFFICIENT, SECURE, AND CONFIDENT

Remember what Eve was to Adam? A helpmeet: to help me meet some stuff. I need some assistance; I mean I need us to be on the same page. I really need you to give me godly advice. A man ought to be able to pick up the phone and say, "Baby, I'm stuck. I don't know what to do." He calls knowing that you have advice and he respects your opinion. So you tell him something, and just by talking with you, he gets a new look at the situation. He's not stuck. He is grateful to have someone in his corner. You are his consultant; the two of you work together, as a team. You give valuable assistance, and he wants you to be the one he calls.

Men and women want to be needed by their mate, but they also want their partner to have a separate identity. Men want a woman to want to be with them out of desire, not desperation—materially or emotionally. They want the woman to be active and independent, to have her own friends and interests. Men don't want your world to revolve around them. That scares us; we can't handle that. As godly men, we assume that when we step to you, you already have something going on. You have your ministry, work, hobbies. Please do not look to live vicariously through us. As healthy men, when we meet you, we don't expect you to drop your interests to devote all that extra time to us.

First Corinthians 9:24-26 talks about running your race with surety and sufficiency. When a good, godly man is out there, he doesn't want to connect with somebody who needs him to take care of her. We need a woman who is secure in God, and who has or is working toward developing her own relationship with God. The issue is that men always want to feel needed by you, but at the same time they want to know that you're not needy.

Women, recognize that there's a fine line between being strong and self-sufficient on one hand and feeling you don't need a man at all on the other. You don't really want or need that person trying to do for you what God can do better anyway. Men aren't created for that. When you come into a new relationship, you should not expect some man to come pay your rent or to help you out with your finances. Remember that he had obligations and responsibilities before meeting you. He doesn't expect to begin financing your basic needs. Often people get into paying bills for their significant other as a form of gift-giving, but that is not appropriate. You are an active, accomplished woman who confidently takes care of her own finances. Even if you get into a financial pinch, you should try to work it out without including your boyfriend in the solution.

10. SHE UNDERSTANDS THE IMPORTANCE OF AFFIRMATION

Just as women have strong emotions, men have strong egos. Just as managing emotions is a struggle for many women, men struggle to manage their egos and they need women to help. In many arenas in society men are bruised and beaten. So they come to women for affirmation. Most men are not trifling, deadbeats, or wife beaters. If you have a man who is loving, holding it down, and doing well, you need to affirm that on a regular basis. He needs to hear that from you! So that when he goes to work and seductive Sally gets in his face with compliments, he can say, "That's just what my wife said this morning. I'll tell her you agree with her. Thank you, though." He won't say, "Really?" When he's affirmed sufficiently at home, he's not hungry for it elsewhere.

11. SHE CAN COOK AND MANAGE THE HOUSE

In this twenty-first century, women *and* men need to know how to care for themselves. But men want a woman who knows how to cook. That may sound old-fashioned, but it is still true. If you don't know how to throw down in the kitchen, take some lessons. With the advances in what we know about nutrition, it's important to know how to prepare healthy foods that will preserve our bodies as temples.

Younger women would do themselves a great service by talking to seasoned women and getting some wisdom on how to manage a home. Because in addition to being supportive and knowledgeable, women need to know how to do a variety of duties: from organizing a formal dinner to managing household repairs to sewing the button on her husband's suit. Hear me now! This does not mean that she has to do all these things, but she should know how.

You may wonder what that has to do with a relationship. In the home, a man is the king and you are queen. So, if he's treating you like a queen, it's easy to do all this stuff, right? If he's treating you right, then when he leaves home, he thinks about the great value of his home and family. Other women who want to put other ideas in his head may confront him. But his response will be, "If you knew what I left at home, you'd get out of my face."

12. SHE VALUES HER APPEARANCE

We know that most women dress to impress other women, not men. And ultimately, we know your focus for your appearance should be yourself and how you want to reflect

God's glory in you. But living in the real world, you also have to consider the fact that men are visual; and just as you want a man to value his physical appearance, you have to value yours. Men do look at your lips, hair, hips, and skin. Yes, they do! Christian men are visual and they are thinking and looking at you. Yes, they value who you are on the inside, but it behooves you to take care of yourself on the outside too.

Of course, a sole focus on beauty is vain. But it's important to understand that God gave the gift of hairdressers for a reason. They can help you; they can save you time, and you know nail techs. Your man—and all other men—don't want to see you out in the mall with hair rollers. And house shoes are just that—shoes you wear inside the house.

The issue is that you really do want to take care of yourself. You may want to think that it doesn't matter that you didn't make it to the hairstylist. That's never true. It does matter how you look. Go the extra mile and make sure that stuff underneath is matching too! You ought to be the finest thing imaginable to your man. If you are married, you ought to be your husband's eye candy. Whether your relationship is new or thirty years old, give your appearance the same attention. Appearance means something and it inspires your man to keep his appearance up for you.

13. SHE KNOWS HOW TO SHARE AFFECTION

This is a biggie—of mammoth proportion. Men don't want you to use affection as a bargaining chip, like when you get mad and shut down the shop. Hebrews 13:4 says this. He really doesn't want somebody else. He wants affection in his marriage. According to 1 Corinthians 7:4, we understand that "the wife hath not power of her own body, but the husband: and likewise also the husband hath not power of his own body, but the wife" (KJV). The marriage bed is to be undefiled.

14. SHE VALUES FIDELITY AND COMMITMENT

Fidelity is a must. I know some of you are shocked and will reread this. Men want fidelity? It's true. Men don't want a woman who has a roaming eye or who can't wholeheartedly commit to the relationship. Many define commitment as fidelity, plus the willingness to work on the relationship— even when the going gets tough. It's interesting that this message in Proverbs is a word of wisdom and warning to a young man to be careful with women who do not have fidelity or who don't understand commitment. When it comes to sexuality and our woman, some men can be incredibly insecure. So when her eyes roam, it sends a specific message to him. Whether she knows or intends this, it highlights his inadequacies and challenges his manhood.

15. SHE KNOWS HOW MEN NEED
TO BE TREATED SEXUALLY

Women, let me tell you something: not all men cheat; but you have to understand what leads to that and understand the process. Men are motivated by their egos. You can take everything from us, but don't be messing with our psyche. We want our importance acknowledged—it may be my car, my degree, social standing in the community, my profession, my fabulous home. It may be none of that. The point is, regardless of my status, recognize who I am, what I'm about, what I can do.

But men aren't going to admit this, so I'm going to say it for them. We live this out in different kinds of ways. When our ego is not properly managed at home, then we begin to look for it to be managed somewhere else. Men think about sex in different ways from women. So when you married that man, you need to understand that he thinks about sex ten times more than you think about it. That man could have a bleeding arm, and you'd say, "We've got to get to the emergency room." He won't say this, but he's thinking, "We'll go after we have sex." When you ask, "Are you hungry?" he's thinking, "After we have sex." You may come to tell him someone's called to say his mother is ill. His verbal response is, "Okay, we'll go see about her right away." Internally, he's thinking, "We'll leave right after we have sex."

The church doesn't address this: how do you deal with this issue with these good, saved men in church? They love God and they're just out of control. I do a lot of marriage counseling, and see many marriages falling apart. But the bottom line reveals that their problems lie in three areas: communication, money, or sex. The Bible tells us that all should honor marriage, and the marriage bed should be kept pure and undefiled. What men want at home is to be completely satisfied sexually by their spouses.

Understand this, sisters: when it comes to your body, men are visual. They may not see the new painting you purchased or the fresh flowers in the kitchen, but when it comes to your body, believe me, they're paying close attention. So wives, please throw the flannels away! Those tacky bedclothes may be comfy for you, but they do nothing for your visual man.

Coming to bed all wrapped up is damaging your marriage. It's the truth! Your husband won't tell you this, but let me help you save your marriage. Sisters, before you get married, you need to understand this: men need to see how beautiful you are. The Bible says you should satisfy him and you've got to take care of yourself.

You've got to know that when your husband leaves the house, the last image he has of you stays with him all day long. Ask yourself, what was the last image my husband had of me this morning? Take care of yourself; fix your hair; hook yourself up. Don't ever get so comfortable or complacent with your husband that you think it's all right if you dress any old way. It may take extra effort, but look at it as your way of honoring and ministering to him. You're treating him and his ego. You've got to make certain that you keep yourself the apple of his eye, because men are visual.

Of course men of God want women who are spiritual; but at the end of the day, that man wants his wife to look good. She needs to look good for him all the time. When she steps out, he wants to be proud of her and brag about her. He feels like announcing, "Hey, that's my wife right there!" That's for his ego! If you don't think this is important, watch out! The fallout from that thinking can be a monster. I'm just trying to save your marriage. Are you all hearing me?

A woman needs to understand that her ministry is to her husband and that sexually—as long as they both agree on the activity, and it causes no harm, humiliation, or pain—nothing is out of bounds. It's your marriage and you need to do what you got to do to save your marriage.

The wise woman builds her house, says the first verse of Proverbs 14, but with her own hands the foolish one tears hers down. That man needs to know you're his number one cheerleader. When that man gets bruised all day long at work, he needs to come home and hear, "Baby, I believe in you. You out there working, making it happen for the family." That woman needs to build him up. Do not tell him how trifling or irresponsible he is. Every man needs to be built up at home, because for most men in our society, the system tears them down every day. A godly wife creates a positive atmosphere in the home and makes sure it is conducive for fruit-bearing productivity (Galatians 5:22-23), a place where her man feels energized when he comes home.

THINK ABOUT THIS

1. Which standards can you easily meet? Which standards do you need to address?

2. Do you think the advice from the wise woman in Proverbs is helpful today? What advice would you add or change?

3. If you were talking to a young person about a woman's role, what would you say?

STEP 3

BE REAL

DON'T USE BASEBALL RULES WHEN YOU PLAY BASKETBALL

You raise your arms up to swing at the ball. You can clearly see the bleachers from where you stand and you intend to knock the ball out of the park. But all your teammates are looking at you funny, because you are at the gym and they want you to score by shooting the ball through the hoop. You are supposed to be playing basketball, not baseball. Knowing what game you are playing and what the rules are makes all the difference. Can you image Kobe running down the court yelling "Steal!" and one of the other guys looking to throw to third base?

RULES OF ENGAGEMENT: RESPONSIBILITY AND ACCOUNTABILITY

We've already talked about trust, honesty, and standards in relationships, and those are also part of what it means to be real, be who you are. But to be real also means that you have to know the rules. Part of being in a relationship that God ordains is playing fair, using the right rules.

The military and police use what they call the rules of engagement. For them these rules determine when, where, and how much force should be used. The rules of engagement provide a consistent, understandable, and repeatable standard. Typically these rules are carefully thought out in detail well in advance and cover a number of scenarios. They allow troops to act in a responsible way as dictated by the chain of command, which in turn holds everyone accountable for their actions. The rules are the standard by which their behavior is judged.

Just for the record, I am not talking about using force in relationships. Violence will destroy a meaningful relationship quicker than anything else. But the rules of engagement that I am talking about do involve responsibility and accountability. It means that when I love somebody, certain rules are tied to that love. Even though I love you, there are certain responses, behaviors, or acts I'm not going to do, because I can't love you and disrespect myself at the same time. Romans 12 teaches that love has rules of engagement. God's love is the paradigm, the model by which I love you.

GOD HAS THE AUTHORITY TO MAKE THE RULES AND HOLD YOU ACCOUNTABLE

God has authority by the nature of who He is. Here are the ways God defines Himself.

- "I am your shield." (Genesis 15:1)
- "I am Almighty God." (Genesis 17:1)
- "I am the LORD." (Exodus 6:6)
- "I, the LORD your God, am a jealous God." (Exodus 20:5)
- "I am gracious." (Exodus 22:27)
- "I am holy." (Leviticus 11:44)
- "I am the First and I am the Last." (Isaiah 44:6)

DEVELOPING YOUR RULES TO LIVE BY

Rules bring order in our lives. They protect us so that we can be real with ourselves and others. They teach us to determine how we'll be treated by others. When we step out of bounds, disorder begins. We have to take control and ownership of our attitudes and beliefs and realize that when we try to take on other people's issues, we delve into territory we are not qualified to handle.

> **When you know what is in and out of bounds in a relationship, you know how to treat others and they know how to treat you.**

God is a God of order, not of confusion. Because of that, when we learn to play by God's rules, we gain a clear sense of what we can expect in a relationship. When I know and articulate my boundaries, it tells other people how to treat me. People know how to step to me because they understand my boundaries.

Without clear, defined boundaries, you can't blame people for how they treat you. But when your standard is God's, you know when they're disrespecting you. You will know your rights and privileges as a child of the King.

DETERMINE WHAT IS IN AND OUT OF BOUNDS

A friend of mine used to live across the street from a golf course. It was not uncommon for players to run across the street and secretly try to drive their golf balls out of the yard rather than take the required penalty shot. Needless to say, my friend's yard was scarred by those golfers trying to hit the green from his yard. One even had the nerve to come up on the porch to retrieve his lost ball. This guy was way out of bounds, trespassing on private property.

When people choose to trespass, it's sort of a test; they're trying to see how strong the boundary is. They are trying to see how much they can get away with. A fence or sign on property is supposed to tell outsiders not to enter without permission. If someone doesn't see the fence and enters anyway, she may say, "Oh I'm sorry. I didn't know I wasn't supposed to be here." And the property owner can then say, "You're forgiven. Now please, step off my property." But if someone jumps over the fence, ignoring the rules, the property owner may have to take stronger steps. For some who continually and intentionally ignore the boundary, it means a lack of respect for you and the rules of engagement.

My staff knows I have a boundary about Mondays. They know not to call me on that day. That's a boundary, because that's my day. It's not *Bishop* Walker day; Monday is *Joseph* Walker day. But if I allow people to break that boundary, that's on me. I can't complain about being stressed out if I allow people to break my boundary. So when you start talking about how stressed out you are or how hard you're working, it may be a sign that it's time to set some boundaries for yourself. But no matter the type of boundary you set, it should be flexible, allowing room to choose what to let in and what to keep out. There are always emergencies and exceptions, even on Joseph Walker Mondays.

HOW DO YOU SET BOUNDARIES?

These suggestions will help you make a good start.

1. *Turn your cell phone off*, especially when you want to be alone or alone with an important person. I know that's oxygen for many of you, but think about it. You need time away to hear your own thoughts, to focus on another person, and to listen for God's voice. That's setting a boundary.

2. *Let people know what is acceptable and unacceptable language to you*. It may mean saying to someone who complains or verbally abuses: "I'm a person of worth; therefore I don't deserve to be a target of your rage." That's a healthy boundary. "I value myself too much to sit up here and take this. I enjoy being with you, but I don't have to go out of my way to make contact with you every day." That's setting a boundary.

3. It may mean saying to someone who is emotionally needy: "I am not responsible for your emotions. I am responsible for my own emotions. I want to hear and understand you, but my thoughts and opinions are important too." That's setting a boundary.

DON'T TRIP 'CAUSE THEY'RE TRIPPIN'

As you set these boundaries, please understand that they are going to be interpreted and misinterpreted by people. Your friends may have a difficult time adjusting to your new boundaries because some people have had a free pass in and out of your life and in and out of your emotions. When people are used to coming at you one way, you can expect them to have difficulty with coming at you in another way. So as people see you setting new boundaries, they're going to struggle with that. Be prepared to stand firm.

FREE TO BE REAL

Rules define what is right and what is wrong. Sally is a gifted musician. As a seven-year-old, she could play the piano like nobody else. In fact, she was almost too talented for her own good, because she thought she even knew better than her teacher. At every lesson the teacher would mark up the music, put in the fingering, mark the dynamics, and send it home for Sally to practice. Sally didn't think she had to follow those silly rules and she made up her own fingering. After all, she was so gifted. Time and again, her teacher tried to explain how using the proper fingers on the keys would enable Sally to play even better. But Sally didn't listen. She didn't listen until she started practicing a piece that she just could not master. After many frustrating lessons, Sally finally paid attention and played with the fingering her teacher suggested. Suddenly, the passage fell into place and Sally could play it now, easily. Sally learned that rules are not just meant to restrict and tell us what not to do but to help us do what we need to do to be successful. In relationships, God gives you rules to live by, not to prevent you from having fun but to free you to be the real you.

THE PHYSICAL YOU

Your skin is a boundary; everything within your skin is the God-given, physical you. But the personal boundary also exists beyond that of your skin, beyond your person. We become aware of this when somebody stands too close to us. According to the cultural rules of this country, we have about an eighteen-inch radius around ourselves that serves as a comfort zone. And if you are a stranger, we expect you to stay outside that invisible eighteen-inch circle. In some countries the circle is smaller. But if you come uninvited into that zone, our comfort level lessens. It's a boundary. That's the reason that getting in someone's face is uncomfortable and intimidating.

THE EMOTIONAL YOU

Emotional boundaries protect us from discomfort and emotional pain. You can't be free to be yourself if you are hurting. These feelings can surface when a co-worker asks you to contribute to their child's school fundraising efforts or when your friend asks to borrow money. Sometimes people just give you TMI (too much information) about their personal life. If you feel uncomfortable when these things happen, your emotional boundaries are being tested. This discomfort is a sign that you need to pay attention and ask yourself why you feel this way.

Guarding your heart (Proverbs 4:23) means not allowing people to trample over you and take advantage of you. If you allow yourself to be used or unduly dependent on someone, it gives people an invitation to come in and try to become what God wants to be for you all along. For example, if your girlfriend *has* to tell you how handsome, strong, and smart you are for you to feel good about yourself, you are too emotionally dependent on her. Or if you are so jealous when your boyfriend even mentions the name of a friend who happens to be a woman, you are too emotionally dependent on him.

Sometimes out of emotional vulnerabilities your heart gets broken. Sometimes other people cannot be there for you or cannot be what you need them to be. A professor told me that one of the signs of being an adult is that you have forgiven your parents for not being

> **No person can perfectly meet your needs; only God can do that.**

what you really needed. One of the signs of a healthy relationship is that your significant other doesn't have to be everything you need him or her to be. No person, no matter how wonderful and real, can perfectly meet your needs; only God can do that.

YOUR SEXUAL BOUNDARIES

A healthy person has sexual boundaries. What is in and out of bounds for you as far as sex is concerned? How do you set this kind of boundary? A great example of how you can set sexual boundaries comes from the story of Joseph. Joseph worked in Potiphar's house (Genesis 39). Potiphar's wife tried to push up on the brother and Joseph said no. In fact he was continually emphatic, something you have to be when setting sexual boundaries. Joseph had an established boundary. Mrs. Potiphar may have been fine and tempting, but he said no. He understood his destiny in that house was greater than three minutes. Unless you understand that what you have is greater than three minutes, you'll never set appropriate sexual boundaries.

Matthew 5:28 says that adultery is out of bounds—not only in action, but also in thought. You can't lust after another man's wife or another woman's husband. That's a boundary. You have to catch yourself when you find you're going too far and ask God's help in the struggle: "Lord, help me now! Jesus, help me now! Now, Lord! Help me be up in your mind, now, Jesus, now."

Romans 1:24-25 says that a lack of boundaries will lead to dishonor and ruin. Not everybody who wants to hug you wants to hug you in Jesus' name. So you have to be sensitive enough in the spirit to know whether people are genuine in their embrace or if they're living out some fantasy. If you're not discerning, you will allow their fantasies to be played out in your naivete.

In your sexual relationship there is a difference between enmeshment and intimacy. Enmeshment may feel like intimacy, but it's not. The word *enmesh* means to catch, trap, or entangle. Enmeshment is attempting to feel and think as if both people in a relationship are the same person. Often, quite a bit of one's uniqueness is missed this way; so neither person is really whole. With intimacy, the experience is completely different. Intimacy comes from knowing each other extremely well, accepting, sharing, and loving each other in spite of shortcomings and differences. Intimacy is between two separate people.

When couples become enmeshed, the personalities of the individual partners are sacrificed for the relationship, and both individuals suffer and begin to feel trapped. In other words, enmeshment says, "You become me and I become you." Intimacy says, "I accept you for who you are; you accept me for who I am. I accept your strengths and weaknesses and you accept mine; we work on the weaknesses together. I can't be you and you can't be me." And oftentimes we go into relationships with people trying to get them to think like us, be like us, but they're not. That's why it's important to be real, set those boundaries, and let people know what they're getting up front. Delilah and Samson are a perfect example. She entangled him in her own issues, pleasing the Philistines, rather than respecting and accepting him without trying to change him.

YOUR SOCIAL CROWD

That old adage is true: "Birds of a feather flock together." Psalm 1 says, "Blessed is the man / Who walks not in the counsel of the ungodly." Counsel suggests advice. So let's read it this way: *Blessed is the one who does not take advice from people who are going contrary to God's will. Blessed is that person who does not stand for what sinners stand for and who does not become comfortable in their mess.* Anybody who wants to achieve any level of success and productivity in a relationship has to be careful about the social crowd. If your significant other takes counsel from ungodly friends, your relationship has a slim chance of success.

One of the things that will mess most people up is not their inside potential; it is not the dreams, not the vision; it's the lack of will to break from the crowd. From counseling many people I've learned the thing that has kept them back so long is not letting let go of their crowd. God delivers them, brings them out of a negative situation, and they feel obligated to go back and be like their old crowd. God saves us so we can bring others up to God, not for them to bring us down to them!

In 1 Thessalonians 5:22, the Bible tells us to shun the very appearance of evil. If it doesn't look right, it can mess you up. Sometimes we do some of the stupidest things in the world. Think about it. Some things just don't look right; it could be innocent, but it doesn't look right. The appearance of evil can get you in more trouble than evil itself.

Proverbs 17:17 gives a good social boundary: "A friend loves at all times." A real friend will tell you when you're wrong, and say to you, "Even if this may cost our friendship, I love you too much to let you do this. So I'm going to tell you about yourself since nobody else will."

THE SPIRITUAL YOU

Knowing who you really are in God and developing your spiritual beliefs will help you determine your spiritual boundaries. To know my spiritual identity, I accept that I am fearfully and wonderfully made and that God makes no junk. I am God's child, phenomenally crafted in God's image. Your ability to interpret my spiritual behavior helps you understand the real me and what rules of engagement I abide by. If we begin to walk like God wants us to walk and to think

Love and Intimacy

like God wants us to think, God promises us that everything we do will prosper (Joshua 1:8). When you are grounded and rooted in the faith of God, you have a foundation from which you can grow and blossom as a healthy person.

> Furthermore then we beseech you, brethren, and exhort you by the Lord Jesus, that as ye have received of us how ye ought to walk and to please God, so ye would abound more and more.
> For ye know what commandments we gave you by the Lord Jesus.
> For this is the will of God, even your sanctification, that ye should abstain from fornication:
> That every one of you should know how to possess his vessel in sanctification and honor. (1 Thessalonians 4:1-4 KJV)

The Scriptures say this is how you ought to walk and to please God. I must walk as He wants me to walk, so I have to value myself as a sanctified vessel, as a temple of God. In a museum, certain items are so valuable that they place a "Do not touch" sign beside them. The greater the value, the fewer people can handle it. You want to carry yourself as though you are expensive, valuable, not passed around from person to person. To be real, you must believe that you have ulti-mate authority over how you are treated. You and only you decide how and when you are touched; you choose how close you will let people come.

Spiritual issues are often tested in doctrinal conversations. The Bible is complex, and heated discussions on various in-terpretations naturally occur. You have to know what healthy debate is, but you also have to give people a sense that they can't get you tripped up over what you believe. Don't allow people to get you in a place where they are trying to uproot everything that you're standing on in faith. By studying the Scriptures, you strive to be rooted and built up in the Word. When you know what you know and why, then you won't need to debate it all day long.

Another facet of spiritual boundaries lies with those enduring spiritual warfare. Spiritual warfare is when demons, fallen spirits, evil people, or impostors attempt to deceive and hinder goodness and the will of God. These attacks can be assaults on a person's thoughts, relationships, and personal relationship with God, or they can be demonic possession or harassment. You may be going through issues of sickness, financial distress, and other tribulation. During these times you have got to have the right people around you and to call upon the prayer warriors of the church. These trials are serious and too difficult to be handled within the confines of a human relationship. You can't just assume that the people you already know will be equipped to handle what you're dealing with.

JESUS AND HIS BOUNDARIES

In Mark 5, Jesus sets some spiritual boundaries. Jairus, a Jewish official, asks Jesus to come home with him because his daughter is ill. While Jesus is on His way to Jairus's house, the woman with the issue of blood interrupts Him. Jesus stops and heals her and as a result of that, time passes. Jairus's people come saying, *It's too late. Your daughter's dead. Why trouble Jesus?* Now watch the boundaries start setting in. "As soon as Jesus heard the word that was spoken, He said to the ruler of the synagogue, 'Do not be afraid; only believe' " (v. 36).

Like Jesus, you have to set a boundary and say *I can't operate unless I know where you are. If I'm coming to your house, I
need you to believe.* That's a spiritual boundary. Jesus is saying,
in verse 36, *I need to know you believe because I can't waste my
time. I just healed a woman. You just saw it. Her faith made her
whole. So if you want this to happen, do you believe?*

Now watch the boundary setup: "And he permitted no one
to follow Him except Peter, James, and John the brother of
James" (v. 37). Now Jesus has twelve disciples, but He only
takes three. Wonder why He doesn't take Bartholomew, An-
drew, and Judas? Thomas and all them? Wonder why? He
knew who was at a level of spiritual maturity to handle it.
Jesus didn't take everybody. It doesn't mean they weren't
good; they just weren't good for or spiritually equipped for
this event. Now, there are some people in your life who are
good; but they aren't necessarily good for this part of your
spiritual journey.

He comes to Jairus's house and He sees the tumult. People
are crying and weeping, wailing greatly. He comes in and
asks: What's the problem? Why are y'all crying so? His next
statement begins another boundary setup: He defines who
He is by saying, "The child is not dead." He's trying to elim-
inate doubters to establish boundaries. They say the girl is
dead; Jesus says she is not dead, which stimulates this response in verse 40: "they laughed Him to scorn" (KJV).

Now, here is something interesting to understand about
church folk: in verse 38 they're crying; in verse 40 they're
laughing. How do you go from all that wailing to laughing?
But watch this: "when He had put them all out" (KJV)—
boundary—*all y'all get out!* They start laughing and Jesus is
like: *Good, I can see right now all y'all need to go; 'cause y'all*

obviously can't stand with me. No faith in here. I've got Peter, James, and John and these believing parents.

Sometimes it's all right to say, "You know what? Right through here, I'm going to have to shut you out. Don't take it personally, but what I need from God is too great for me to have you in here. I'll be back to you directly." You may be going through stuff right now and some folk laughing at you for believing in and waiting on God. They are not standing with you and yet they wonder why you're not calling them back. You have to shut them out during this period of your life.

So the Bible says that Jesus took the father, the mother, Peter, James, John, right? Six people and the girl, that's seven, a complete room. We got six of them and one Jesus. And the Bible says, "He took the child by the hand, and said to her, 'Talitha, cumi,' which is translated, 'Little girl, I say to you, arise.' " And immediately she stood up and walked around. They were astonished, completely blown away! Jesus gave them strict orders not to let anyone know about this miracle and told them to feed the girl.

When you are in need of a breakthrough, you got to begin to evaluate your crowd and determine—through prayer—who can come to that level of faith with you and believe God for what you need. When you have the right people in the right place at the right time and God is there, miracles happen! And the biggest miracle is that you can be real, your real self, with the person who matters most.

WHEN THE REAL YOU NEEDS A LIFT

As real as we may be and as much as we play by the rules, sometimes life is not fair. We get hurt and sometimes we just can't drop our baggage. Can you imagine running the hundred-yard dash or the 4x4 relay carrying around a couple of fifty-pound suitcases? Or can you imagine jumping those hurdles, dragging a couple of hefty briefcases? It would be a funny picture, if it wasn't so sad. But in everyday life, people carry heavy burdens all the time.

Experiences have molded and shaped us into the people we are today. It doesn't matter if you have a Bible as big as a ghetto blaster or a colossal cross around your neck or if you live a minimalist life, no amount of masking or camouflage will hide your issues. Even if you think you hide it well, eventually the truth will come out. We've been taught that Christians are supposed to be the encouragers and sometimes we think that salvation ensures we'll automatically know how to cope with problems, obstacles, and challenges. But life is not that easy. When people ask us how we're doing, we may say, "Praise the Lord, hallelujah." But deep down inside we're wrestling with some stuff. Behind our praise, there's pain that potentially blocks us from living as fully as God intended.

You need to know that we serve a God who is able to deliver us from private pain regardless of what has happened or what somebody has done to you. You don't have to fake it another day. You can't fake it and be real at the same time. You don't have to act like you're doing fine when you're not. You know you can't fix it if you don't face it first. But you won't face it alone; you have God to help you. God is getting ready to move you from your pity party, out of that state of depression. When you recognize who you are in Him, God will move you from private pain to public praise. He will give you the power to face your issues and lay those suitcases down for good.

LOVE TRIANGLE: JACOB, LEAH, AND RACHEL

> And he went in also unto Rachel, and he loved also Rachel more than Leah, and served with him yet seven other years. And when the LORD saw that Leah was hated, he opened her womb: but Rachel was barren.
>
> And Leah conceived, and bare a son, and she called his name Reuben: for she said, Surely the LORD hath looked upon my affliction; now therefore my husband will love me.
>
> And she conceived again, and bare a son; and said, Because the LORD hath heard that I was hated, he hath therefore given me this son also: and she called his name Simeon.
>
> And she conceived again, and bare a son; and said, Now this time will my husband be joined unto me, because I have born him three sons: therefore was his name called Levi.
>
> And she conceived again, and bare a son: and she said, Now will I praise the LORD: therefore she called his name Judah; and left bearing. (Genesis 29:30-35 KJV)

This is the story of Jacob, Rachel, and Leah. It is a love triangle. On the run from his brother, Esau, Jacob arrives at his Uncle Laban's house. His uncle allows him to stay, and Jacob promises to work for his uncle while he stays there. His uncle says, "Because you are my flesh and blood, I won't let you work for nothing. What would you like?" Remembering how stunning Rachel is, Jacob immediately answers, "I'll work seven years for Rachel, your daughter." So Laban agrees and the deal is set.

Now Jacob is a trickster; he is known for getting over on people. He tricked his twin brother, Esau, out of his inheritance—that's why he was on the run. But trickstering runs in the family, and Jacob is about to meet his match.

At the end of seven years the wedding is set. The preparations are all made, the fatted calf is on the roast. Then comes the wedding night; naturally Jacob thinks he is going to bed with Rachel, his new wife. The marriage will be con-summated and everyone will live happily ever after. How-ever, when he pulls the covers back, he doesn't see Rachel. Instead he sees her sister, Leah. Jacob has been outfoxed by his uncle, now father-in-law. The player got played. I don't care how smooth you think you are, I don't care how you think you can get over, there's always somebody else more cunning than you. Jacob storms in to Laban, "What's going on? I thought I was marrying Rachel."

But Uncle Laban explains that according to custom, the older daughter has to marry before the younger. So Jacob says, "Well, if that's so, then give me Rachel now and I will work an additional seven years for her." The uncle agrees and gives Rachel to Jacob with the understanding that Jacob will work an additional seven years to pay for her. So you have Jacob with two wives, one he dislikes and one he adores. You have two women, sisters, competing for the love of one man; one rela-tionship is born out of cultural requirements and expectations, and the other is born out of physical attraction and love.

How did this affect Leah? What does it mean to be picked over? What does it mean to be the one who comes in second? Leah's humiliation is certain, but we also understand this kind of pain and what it meant for both Leah and Rachel.

WHAT'S IN A NAME?

Leah's name in Hebrew means *weary, grieved, offended*— even *impatient*. Rachel's name means *ewe, lamb of God*, pos-sibly *innocence and gentility of a rose*, or *lovely*. Leah is injured because, although older, she is in the shadow of her sister; she's considered the ugly duckling. When people want to go out, they say, "We want Rachel. We don't want to deal with her sister, Leah. Rachel's got it going on." Leah's issues stem from her physical appearance, contrasted with Rachel's. The Bible says Leah is tender-eyed or cross-eyed (Genesis 29:17). Even though she is older, she's a step behind her sister and this has damaged her self-esteem.

GOD-GIVEN VALUE

Leah's problem was that she was not in touch with who she really was; she was not in touch with her own value, her own self-worth. Truthfully it is difficult for us to measure Leah by our twenty-first–century standards because a lot of her self-worth was compounded by the nature of her culture and the expectations and value her society placed on women. In that time, a woman's value was a small step above an ox. She was a piece of property. So if she had much value at all, it would be found in her appearance and in her ability to produce male children. Laban knew no one would ever ask for Leah in marriage, so he devised a plan to unload her on Jacob. What neither Laban nor Jacob knew at the time of the marriage was that even though Leah was not beautiful or even loved, she would produce many sons. And from one of her sons would come Jesus. Her value was God-given.

NO JUNK FROM GOD

When you realize who you are in God and who God has made you, you don't have to live your life trying to impress somebody else. Today's women are constantly told—by society, by the media, by a variety of people—that they are too fat, too skinny, too black, too weak; that they are ugly, stupid,

> **God made us and God does not make junk.**

dumb, unimportant, and expendable. But we must all understand that it's not how people label us that makes us who we are, it's who we answer to and under whose rules we live—the standards we uphold. God made us and God does not make junk. That's why we have to understand that greater is God within us than the one who is within the world.

THE REAL DEAL

I know God made me just like He wanted me to be. He made my head like He wanted my head. He made my feet like He wanted my feet. He made your hips like He wanted your hips, He made your lips like He wanted your lips. If folk have a problem with how God made you, you tell them to go the other way, that you are going your way, and may the Lord watch over you both while you are absent from one another.

Have you been torn up, balled up, spit on, thrown down, and stepped on by negative relationships? Do you feel you've been passed from person to person? God told me to tell you that you've not lost your value! High-five somebody and tell them, "You don't know what I've been through, but thank God I haven't lost my value!"

YOU ARE BLESSED AND HIGHLY FAVORED

One of the keys to unlocking the prison bars of low self-esteem is knowing that God favors you. It makes no difference how people feel about you. *Get comfortable with the fact that you are blessed and highly favored.* Favor is that energy that gets you the parking space when everybody else is still driving around. Favor is that privilege that gets you a seat in the restaurant while others are told there's an hour wait. It's that approval that gets you the house when your credit report said you could have it; it's that grace that comes when you receive an encouraging card or phone call from someone you had no clue was thinking of you.

Leah had a self-esteem issue. The Bible says that God favored Leah even though Jacob preferred her sister. Rachel had position, but Leah had function. God favored Leah by opening her womb, giving her a perfect opportunity to birth a blessing. But, because she was in love with somebody who was paying her no attention, she took the gift God intended to be a blessing and she birthed burdens.

It's also interesting to see how the meaning of names reflects the family's story. Typically, Hebrew names describe a situation or circumstance; they're a descriptive statement about who the person is. So usually what a person is called describes an attribute or characteristic of that person or what the person's family was experiencing at the time of the birth.

Leah got Jacob's attention and she communicates to Jacob through her children. The first child is named Reuben, which means *to look* or *to see*. She's thinking maybe now Jacob will see her and maybe when he sees Reuben, he'll take his eyes off Rachel and see only Leah.

WHAT IS YOUR REUBEN?

What do you use to get people to notice you? Is it the car you drive? Is it the skirt or shorts or the thong you wear? I'm writing this to let you know, that doesn't work. When Reuben didn't get Jacob's attention, Leah had another baby, whom she named Simeon, meaning *to hear*. She's thinking, "If you will not see me, then you will hear me."

WHAT IS YOUR SIMEON?

Who do you want to hear you? Do you page them all day? Do you leave messages on the voice mail all day and all night? Do you argue with them all the time? I'm writing this to let you know, that won't work. So when Simeon's birth makes no difference to Jacob, Leah has baby Levi, whose name means *to be joined*. This time she's plotting that "when Jacob sees this baby, maybe he will want to be connected to me."

WHAT IS YOUR LEVI?

How do you get people to connect with you? Do you think that by buying them things they'll want to be joined to you? Do you think if you offer your apartment and pay the utility bills that they'll want to marry you? Remember that line about people not paying for the cow when they can get the milk for free?

Unknown to Leah, she is making progress in her relationship with God and finally she realizes that having babies won't make Jacob love her. And let me just throw this out parenthetically in case you are paying attention: Don't have a baby to get married! And don't get married just because you had a baby! If you made one mistake, don't make two! Just because you made a mistake and brought a baby into this world, it doesn't mean the father is your soul mate! "Who that is?"

"That's just my baby-daddy." Some people are going through hell right now because they married their baby's daddy.

The Bible says that after Leah suffered through her private pain, struggling to please Jacob and having no love to show for it, she finally gets it in Genesis 29:35. Leah finally realizes that everything she is and everything she has is not because of Jacob, the children, Rachel, her father, or anyone else; it's because of God. She thinks, "Rather than live my life trying to please and impress somebody who doesn't even care about me, this time I will praise the Lord." She realizes she's made many deposits but gotten no returns. She understands "rather than do that, I want to live my life for God."

You finally get it and say: *This is it! This gig is up! I'm not paying another rent payment while you lie on my couch and eat my food. I'm not paying another cell phone bill. I'm living my life for God, not for you!*

The Bible says the name of her last son, Judah, means *praise*. It signifies the end of her plotting. Leah has been at Jacob's house more than she's been at God's house. Now she's gonna praise God for everything she's been through and give it all to God.

WHAT IS YOUR JUDAH?

What are you ready to give over to God so God's grace will saturate your soul so that you offer God praise? What have you surrendered that you can now give God the glory for and say, "I'm living my life for God alone and not for others"? What was Leah's testimony? With all she'd gone through, she tricked herself trying to trick a trickster, but she grew up in God.

I love watching the Tennessee Titans. A few years ago we had a wonderful player named Eddie George. He was great not so much because he ran fast or because he scored a lot of touchdowns. What made Eddie George a great football player was his ability to accumulate YACs. Y-A-C is an acronym for Yards After Contact. When Eddie George held the football deep in his stomach and ran toward a goal, if the opponent hit him he didn't go down. They may have hit him on the 40-yard line, but he didn't go down at the initial point of contact. After he was hit, Eddie had enough strength and stamina to keep moving so that he was able to get down to the 35-yard line—that's five more yards after he had been hit. Do you have a blessing you're holding? Did the enemy hit you when you were young but you are still holding on to God's promise for you? You kept on getting yards after contact?

Leah's testimony was that through it all she stayed faithful and was able to praise God through her circumstances. She could say, "I've been through it and I'm still here. I've been lied to, talked about, criticized, but I'm still here. I've endured so much, I should be walking the streets talking to myself. But when I look at what God has done in my life, I've got a praise inside of me."

One more question.

WHO IS YOUR JACOB?

Who do you need to let go of and, in faith, step away from so you can embrace the blessings God has for you? For you, today may be a time of letting go of Jacob. Leah can tell you that God is looking for total surrender. Use Leah's lesson and stop making the wrong deposits that leave you no returns. Let God know whatever you need. God not only gives us what we need, He gives who we need. Surrender and you will move from your private pain into the real, authentic person God created you to be.

THINK ABOUT THIS

1. How did you get your name? What is the story behind it? Do you have a nickname? Is there a story behind how you got it?

2. Have you ever had a trick played on you? What happened?

3. What happens when a person manipulates a relationship?

4. Where do you need God to lift you up?

BE ON THE SAME TEAM

I am the rose of Sharon, and the lily of the valleys.

As the lily among thorns, so is my love among the daughters.

As the apple tree among the trees of the wood, so is my beloved among the sons. I sat down under his shadow with great delight, and his fruit was sweet to my taste.

He brought me to the banqueting house, and his banner over me was love. (Song of Solomon 2:1-4 KJV)

Once you have found your true love, the one person you are committed to, you begin to think of yourself in terms of how the two of you will live as a couple. You have asked God to bless you with this person and believe God is doing just that. In many ways you are relieved because with this person you are stronger, more ready to face the world. You are looking forward to being a family, to being a unit, a team. But do you know that even the pros have to learn to work as a team for the maximum effect?

I enjoy watching football. It amazes me how teams spend time in the huddle getting their plays together before they come to the line of scrimmage. The basic idea is that each player gets a clear understanding of the play and knows his role—if one player is off-side, the entire team is penalized, and if the running back scores, the entire team has contributed to the touchdown. The tackle blocks and the fullback clears the way. The team's successes and failures are often determined by what happens in the huddle. As a couple it is important that you and your mate spend quality time in the huddle communicating and encouraging each other before entering the line of scrimmage and running the plays of life. Each person strives individually so that together they can achieve their full potential. When you think of the challenges and problems of the world, you feel better equipped to face them with your permanent mate.

Your belief that "God so loved the world that He gave His only begotten Son, that whoever believes in Him should not perish but have everlasting life" (John 3:16) is the blueprint by which the two of you allow yourselves to be loved. You both measure the way you love by this paradigm. Each of you honors the other by this standard. One does not come down to the other's level; the two of you strive to live and love up to God's level. That's why the Bible says, "Husbands, love your wives, just as Christ also loved the church" (Ephesians 5:25). God's unconditional love becomes the paradigm for your relationship.

Solomon compares the love of God to human relationships. As you grow into your relationship, you know that you still live in the real world. You both have good and bad days, but at the end of any day, you are happy to be in each other's presence. You learn to listen to and read your mate's behavior and actions. You can tell when he or she needs something positive, especially in negative situations. When one of you is dealing with drama—whether it comes from forces outside or within—you pray for a God-inspired solution. You know how to look for a positive spin on the situation that will build up your partner. But even on your worst days, you can still be committed to being a team member. Being on the same team means showing up even if you don't feel like it.

Solomon says the love of God creates a positive atmosphere when a negative environment exists. He declares that this kind of love is strong. Whatever you need, God says, "I am there." The revelation here is that God becomes the antithesis, or the very opposite, of what you're going through. The rose of Sharon is a beautiful plant in a terrible place. It is a good thing in a bad place. The lily among thorns represents a remarkable thing to focus on even when life seemingly is being choked out by obstacles and complications. Regardless of the situation, God's love transcends my context.

SEE ME, HEAR ME, BE JOINED WITH ME

This is how we love and how we want to be loved: when I'm going through a negative pasture, my wife or husband treats me in such a way that I get lost in how she or he cares for me and the negative forces around me are weakened. When we think about the goodness of the Lord, we can be in the midst of hell and still be happy. When we think about how much God loves us, we can walk among haters and among people who don't like us and say, "This is the day the LORD has made; / We will rejoice and be glad in it" (Psalm 118:24). We—as a secure couple—rest naturally in the belief that God loves us so much; that belief gives us peace.

Knowing that you are loved and accepted in an intimate, godly relationship will bring you happiness. You can be on your stressful job or in a distressing situation and still say, "Lord, you've been good to me. I thank you and bless your name. It doesn't make a difference what's happening around me, I bless your name because you're doing more for me than they're doing to me."

Here it is: When you're on the same team, there is a way the two of you treat and love each other that shifts your attention away from anything that is distracting or distressing. You learn how to examine a negative situation and not let it take over your spirit. You trust that God will send you the solution, the peace, or the tools to deal with the situation and you both know how to wait for God's intervention. In the meantime, you count your blessings, knowing that God is in control. This may take some practice and some willingness to be patient, but waiting on the Lord will do wonders for your relationship.

> When you're on the same team, there is a way the two of you treat and love each other that shifts your attention away from anything that is distracting or distressing.

If every time your husband calls, there's something wrong, always some drama, that ought to be a sign that he is bringing too many negative issues into your journey. If every time she talks to you, she disrespects you, that is a sign that she didn't talk to God and brought it to you instead. If you're married, then it's time that you both get on your knees and take it to the Lord in prayer. If you are unmarried and you see that your significant other doesn't rely on God, you have to say, "Look, I need somebody in my life who's going to be positive. I'm going through enough hell by myself. I need to feel that when you call me, there will be something pleasant or meaningful and not feel like, 'Uh-oh! Here we go again.' I want to jump in excitement, not cringe whenever I think I'll see you." Solomon expresses that just as the apple tree is unique, unlike any other tree, I am unlike anybody else. In the real sense, I need you to know that you are dealing with a unique, God-fearing, God-depending individual.

When you're growing as a couple, you learn to be perceptive to your lover's needs. "I sat down under his shadow with great delight, and his fruit was sweet to my taste." Any child of God can attest to the fact that whatever you're going through, God knows all about it. God is sensitive to our needs. Solomon came to a point where his past experiences had begun to affect his present situation. God was aware of that and God made him feel secure. God can also help you be more sensitive to your mate's needs.

COMMUNICATION WITHOUT CONSEQUENCE

One of the major problems in relationships is communication without consequence. Many relationships fail because the two are not talking; or if they talk, they avoid the real issues. Sometimes, even after marriage, one person feels afraid to let the other know something about themselves that they aren't proud of. Once you are in a committed relationship, you do not have the luxury of keeping information to yourself. The two of you are now one, not one person, but one team. The Bible says Adam and Eve were naked and not ashamed; they had total disclosure. They were able to share without fear of consequences.

Here's the reality: we experience real love when we go to God's throne. We can tell God who we are and be totally honest. We have no secrets with God. In human relationships, it's riskier because the other person isn't all-knowing or totally forgiving like God, but that's where trust in that person and faith in ourselves comes into the equation. We have to trust that when we reveal our innermost self to the person we love, we will be treated like God treats us. He or she knows that's how God listens and forgives, and we want that same response when we expose our flaws. This is how we love each other: I provide the security you need and vice versa. I can expose the pain of my past and know you got my back.

But people are not like God. And their love and forgiveness will always be conditional to some extent. But love and forgiveness, like hope and faith, grow and deepen the more time we spend with God, because the more time we are with God, the more we become like Him. So if you want to be more loving and if you want your mate to be more accepting, spend more time studying the Word and in prayer.

MUTUAL SACRIFICE, MUTUAL GOALS

Ultimately, God allows your destiny to be hooked up with somebody else's destiny—just like God hooked up our human destiny with His son, Jesus. What Jesus did matters, because His destiny was connected to ours. What you do matters, because your destiny is connected to those you love. When you team up with God, your relationship as a couple will produce fruit for God's kingdom. If you don't think about and value your future, you set out on an untrustworthy path for yourself, your mate, and your children.

The dynamics of married life and of becoming a team for God and for your immediate family means that the two of you are connected, have similar values and goals. You want to grow together. You want to spend your lives serving God together. You even see your connection as a positive force, representing God as you serve one another, family members, your church, and your community. The two of you actively seek ways you can be used by God.

HIS BANNER OVER US IS LOVE

When a football team runs onto the field before the game, they often run through or under a banner with the team's name and logo as a way to promote and inspire the team. For Christian couples, we run onto the field of life under God's banner of Love. Promoting you and your spouse is in God's nature. Verse 4 of our Song of Solomon passage says, "He brought me to the banqueting house, and his banner over me was love." The essence of how God loves us is to make us look good in the world, not just for our own sake, but also for the sake of the team.

But until we understand sacrifice, we can't really love. Solomon says God took him somewhere. God loves us and God proved it by the sacrifice of His son, Jesus. While God sacrificed for us, He also brought Solomon to the

> **Sacrifice and love go hand in hand.**

banqueting house, the house of feasting, the house of abundance. This is the image: God brings you to an expensive event, taking you to the head table as a VIP, and offering you anything you want. You are royalty; you are a royal priesthood—God is saying, whatever you want, I got it. As a team member you will be called upon to take one for the team, but the banquet after the game is worth every sacrifice you make.

God doesn't mind going over and beyond because it's God's nature. God is exceedingly generous. God wants us to have the best. As we grow toward spiritual maturity, we don't mind going over and beyond because as we imitate God, it becomes our nature too. God is good and good is God. We can't separate the goodness from God or God from the goodness. So when we say good, we can only mean God; if we say God, we can only mean good.

When a boxer comes to his corner at the end of a round and sits down, he needs a towel, water, encouragement, and good coaching. He needs his team. He doesn't need to be hit over the head or knocked out between rounds. It's too much to ask for a person to go out and fight in the workplace and have to fight at home. But disagreements will happen. That is normal and natural. But even in your arguments, fight fair. Look to the admonition in Romans 12:10, "Be devoted to one another. . . . Honor one another above yourselves" (NIV). It applies to all situations and in all types of relationships. A wife is devoted to and honors her husband, acknowledging the gifts and anointing upon his life even when she disagrees with him. She doesn't see him like other people see him. She praises his righteousness just as she praises God daily (Psalm 35:28). A husband is devoted to and honors his wife even when he disagrees with her. He acknowledges her gifts and anointing. He doesn't see her as other people see her. He praises her righteousness just as he praises God daily, and he thanks God that he has a righteous wife. So it works both ways: husbands and wives celebrate and praise each other even when it's difficult, even while they disagree. They lift up and encourage each other and listen to each other. They air their views openly without sucker punches. They help each other and are not a hindrance. Honor your spouse by supporting the visions and dreams of your team even when you fight.

Learning to be on the same team begins when you are dating. If the man shares with you the deep matters of his life—bares his soul, telling you his issues and struggles—he needs to know that you will not hold those things against him. Just as you need to feel safe, he needs to feel safe and covered in your confidence. This also means that when he does this, you're not going to be on the phone the next minute with your girlfriends, saying, "Girl, you wouldn't believe what he just told me." Because when you do that, the next time he's around your friends, he wonders why they look at him strangely. Then he realizes that they know something about him.

Men, keeping confidences is necessary for you too. Lift your mate up to God, because if you drag her down, you are dragging yourself down too. If you find you have to tell somebody, go into your closet and speak of the confidence to the Holy Spirit. That is the extent of your sharing that confidence. When you have done that, you can accept the peace the Holy Spirit gives and know that you have honored your mate and lived up to the trust he or she has in you.

I'VE GOT YOUR BACK

As your teammate, I understand your values and goals; I hear and respect your dreams; I see the journey you are undertaking. Because I love you I want you to succeed, and I am willing to sacrifice and talk through our difference. Are you all hearing this? Naked and not ashamed. When I have any opportunity to help you reach your goals, know that I will do all I can, with God's help, to support your dreams and goals. I got your back, just as you have mine. I make sacrifices for you and you make sacrifices for me because we know it will be toward the good for both of us.

When you love me, it ought to be in your nature to want me to have the best. I'm not talking about trying to compete with the Joneses down the street; I'm not even talking about the best there is; but it ought to be clearly evident to me that you've given me your very best.

Think about the essence of how God loves us and the amazing way God provides for us. And what do we give in exchange for that? If that convicts you, don't worry about it. Just drop your head and say, "You got me, Bishop." You don't want your husband or your wife to feel as though you don't do enough for them, or that when you finally do something it doesn't really make an impact because it's been so long coming. You know that if they had to drop several hints or beg for it, when you finally gave in, it meant nothing and the effect was lost.

God blesses you with your relationship. Doesn't it blow your mind how God keeps blessing you knowing you don't deserve it? God's generosity at the banqueting table reminds us of Psalm 23, which says God "prepare[s] a table before me in the presence of my enemies." God hooked me up and I can imagine at the table enemies were there, but I thank God He brought me to the table. God even blesses you in front of your enemies through your relationship with your spouse.

God spoils me. His banner over me is love. Everywhere I go, people know I'm blessed because I have stuff I don't deserve. It's nothing but the goodness of God. You can look at me and tell I'm loved. When you treat me right, you will benefit from all that love God has poured into me. When I look at how God loves you, I stand secure. His banner over you is love. Together we let neither heights, depths, powers, principalities, things present, nor things to come separate us from the love of God that is in Christ Jesus (Romans 8:38-39). God is so confident about how He loves us that God is not insecure in His love. He's so confident in how He loves us and how He hooks us up.

When you truly love right the one you say you love, you won't be insecure. You can know she's with her friends and not be calling in five minutes wondering what she's doing, because you know what's behind her good love. When your man goes out with his boys, you won't trip, because you know he's yours and he knows you are his. When someone tries to step to you, it's really no issue. You confidently say, "No thank you. I promise you, I'm cool. I appreciate all that, but trust me, I am totally satisfied with my spouse." Because you understand that's the love of God living through your relationship. When you come to this level in your relationship, it's amazing, because your standard gets higher. You know that your relationship is powered by a higher source. And you are committed to keep it that way. The more we promote God, the more He promotes us! The more we give to Him, the more He gives to us. But He will love us, no matter what. If you really want to know how to love each other, love like Jesus with your whole self.

Jesus ought to be the center of everything in our lives. We measure every relationship by the love we have for Jesus Christ. He puts clapping in our hands and running in our feet. He makes us smile when nothing is funny. When we think about the goodness of Jesus and all He's done for us, as a team, as a blessed couple, we know we are indeed blessed and highly favored. We confidently go forward in our new family knowing God's been too good to us. We start living like we're sitting at God's banqueting table because God's banner over us is Love!

TAKING TURNS:
WHO GETS TO BE THE LEADER?

Marilyn and Don have been happily married for many years. They are that couple who still enjoys each other's company. One thing that people notice about them is that they don't take themselves too seriously, but without question they are serious about and dedicated to each other. When they go to the movies, Don admits he doesn't really connect with the characters and Marilyn has to explain what's really going on. It's like she uses a second language with him and then he gets it. Marilyn is a musician and performs at local venues; Don accompanies her as her supporter; he sometimes helps out as her assistant before performances. One of Don's strengths is in providing for their family. With the finances and organizing the fundamental maintenance of their home, Don is on it. Marilyn doesn't have to give it a second thought. When they go on vacation, he's got the trans-portation and travel plans organized, almost to a seamless science. Their vacation experience is usually fun and stress-free because he's covered the bases. They each have strengths that give the other freedom and a sense of pride.

Whatever the gifts and talents with couples, each one has strengths and weaknesses. When one person's strengths are called upon, the other supports and lets that person take the lead. There is no wrangling for position or ego-tripping be-cause they see themselves as a complete unit on this journey called life. When one person's acumen on a topic or project is called for, the other person assists and the outcome is pleas-ant and beneficial.

Success in marriage is achieved as each person learns the strengths and weaknesses of the other and together they compensate so that the need is met. Whether deciding where in the world to live, purchasing a home, deciding on educa-tional options for children, determining how much income is reserved for savings or medical needs, or whatever it may be, the capabilities and effectiveness of each person come into play. When one person is not as accomplished as the other, they take the team approach, so that neither person is considered more or less important.

When a challenge or obstacle surfaces, they sit down together and have a healthy discussion. Because they know each other's abilities, the one who is less experienced is ready to bend because he or she knows the other will take the lead in solving this problem or speaking to the issue. They agree that both are working for the good of the family. The phrase "what's yours is mine and what's mine is yours" is the mindset. One person's excellence makes both better.

They each strive to make the other proud and, even though they've been married for quite a few years, they still try to impress each other. Harmony is their goal. And with the harmony comes the effort to keep laughter a part of their equation. They know how far laughter goes, especially in the face of an obstacle that neither can conquer—either alone or together. They also know and depend on God's love and support of their union. They know that being united in God is the thing that makes their family unit stronger and that they can withstand the trials of living because of the One they serve.

When you are on the same team, one person's victory is the other person's and one person's sacrifice is the other person's as well. Together we live under the banner of God's love, working together to bring in God's kingdom.

THINK ABOUT THIS

1. Give an example of communication without consequence. How can you avoid communication without consequence in your relationship?

2. How should a godly couple disagree?

3. Give an example of when humor saved the situation.

4. Many marriages involve going over and beyond. What happens when one person goes over and beyond a lot more than the other? How can couples balance that?

LIVE TO THE GLORY OF GOD TOGETHER

WHAT ARE YOU LIVING FOR?

In the movie *Why Did I Get Married?* Terry and Diane are a couple of married people who struggle with the demands of maintaining successful businesses and nurturing their relationship. While they are on vacation, Diane thinks nothing of taking calls from her office—regardless of what she and Terry are doing. When she learns that Terry has intercepted a call and asked her assistant not to call again so they can have a stress-free vacation, Diane blows up and accuses him of sabotaging her career. She believes her commitment to her job shows how she values their marriage. He feels she is abandoning him and his needs for her work. What are they living for? Their jobs, their selfish desires, each other?

Your relationship is an adventure, and as the years pass there will be new experiences. That's part of the miracle of life and that is worth living for. Just as people mature and change, so will your relationship. Some have said that every seven years the marriage takes on a different texture or personality—just as people change and grow, physically and spiritually. If no change occurs, it is a sign that your marriage is stagnant and probably dying. Some of that change comes as a result of positive experiences; some of it comes because of trials and tribulations. The Bible says that patience comes with tribulations. The blessing is to live through the changes and watch as your relationship blossoms and matures through faith and confidence in God.

Many of us are busy without understanding totally the business that God has given us to do. We are easily consumed with activity and doing good deeds, but we are not taking care of ourselves; we isolate ourselves from family and neglect other responsibilities. We are working for the Lord, but not working with the Lord.

Proper perspective with God in Christ is to work with Him, not so much for Him. It's important to have times of relaxation so tiredness and discouragement cannot settle in, because when they do, you lose perspective. Once you lose perspective, you lose purpose, which births spiritual weariness.

Let's be honest, a lot of folk are just tired. Spiritual weariness is a signal for the enemy to come into your life and cause the very thing God intended to bless you to be a burden. Weariness robs you of your vision and purpose, because you are caught up in the "right now." Remember this acronym: H-A-L-T. Hungry. Angry. Lonely. Tired. Whenever you are hungry (spiritually and physically), angry, lonely, or tired, the enemy uses that as a foothold to come in and to seduce you toward demonic purposes.

> Therefore seeing we have this ministry, as we have received mercy, we faint not;
> But have renounced the hidden things of dishonesty, not walking in craftiness, nor handling the word of God

deceitfully; but by manifestation of the truth commending ourselves to every man's conscience in the sight of God. (2 Corinthians 4:1-2 KJV)

Each of you has a ministry. You have a ministry, not because you are a preacher or pastor, but because you are God's chosen instrument. So when I see my purpose, my ministry, the thing I do every day, my job, my assignment, whatever it is that I feel God has called me to do, I have to put that in proper perspective.

If I lose heart, if I am not productive in the vision or the assignment that God has trusted me with, there has to be a reason why. If I am starting projects and not finishing them, there's a reason why. If there is disorder in my personal life, I have to get to the source. So ministry is hard work. You should view your job and your school as places for ministry. Your ministry is what God has you doing right now.

Here's the challenge: in addition to our ministry we have other relationships to manage. Married people have to organize and protect their time so they can honor the marriage. Single people in relationship have to manage that. Then you manage other relationships: friends, co-workers, church members, relatives, and others. So here's the issue: it's important to know that any time you are in a relationship, investments must be made through your time, service, gifts, and presence.

If the thing that you are doing is draining everything out of you, you will go home or to that relationship as empty, like the empty pitcher on the counter. You won't have anything to pour into that relationship! Now watch this with your equally yoked self: your significant other is also working their ministry, doing what God called them to do, loving God trying to do it. They left home as a full pitcher just like you.

Now they come home empty and you come home empty and you're both—in the name of Jesus—saying:

You: Pour into me.
Her/Him: You pour into me.
You: You pour into me.
Her/Him: No, you pour into me.
You: I got nothing to give. I'm tired. Let's go to sleep.
Her/Him: I don't want to talk, I don't want to do nothing, leave me alone. I don't want the dog to bark, I don't want the cat to meow, the phone to ring, just leave me alone. 'Cause I have nothing to give.

As mature people of God, you both know something's fundamentally wrong. That can't be the quality of life Jesus said He came to give. You know that's why divorce rates are so high among churchgoers. People are working hard, nurturing and developing these life-changing ministries in church, and when they get home they got nothing to give. They are on every mentoring ministry, but their own children suffer—all in the name of Jesus. How the mighty do fall!

Check the scenario: The husband desires respect and intimacy; this is a need the husband brings. He comes home feeling: "I'm the man and I have needs." The wife desires provision too. She's feeling: "Take care of me, honor me, cherish me. I want to feel valued. Talk to me; tell me I'm beautiful."

He comes home empty with expectations and is disappointed because now he doesn't feel she respects him. He's too tired to do the things that she needs to feel intimate. She doesn't feel he's taking care of things and believes he doesn't really appreciate what she does. He doesn't think she understands how he's trying to hold all this stuff together. They both think: "Let's go meet with Bishop Walker."

Once expectations aren't met and new disappointments spring up daily, a loss of respect for each other occurs. She says: "I don't respect you anymore. I sit up in church and watch you do all this stuff for Jesus. I watch you as the pastor's aide, getting Bishop Walker water and you ain't brought me a glass of water in five years."

This is so real. When a lack of respect settles in, a lack of gratefulness comes with it. At this point anything he or she does has no impact. It's too late. Then resistance to sexual intimacy follows. They don't know each other. You know that song, "There's a stranger in my house . . . and it's you."

By now estimation of personal worth comes into question. She's beginning to wonder what she's worth to him. He's wondering if she cares about his needs. The children are thinking, but not saying it aloud, "Are we worth anything, Daddy? The only image I remember of you is the back of your head as you go to work." "Momma, I know you got a boyfriend, but what about my school play?" All in the name of Jesus.

Sometimes there's a surface attempt to improve things, but transparency remains awkward and difficult. They go to the marriage counselor or meet with the pastor because they want to look like they are trying to work it out. It's very awkward because nobody wants to deal with the core issues; nobody wants to be transparent about what's really going on. For couples who have careers and work in ministry, the church is the last place they want to be real. They want folk to think they're really holding it together. They are more concerned about image than integrity.

Now that disappointment is the norm, resentment builds and bitterness is as thick as a brick. The things that once blessed them are now hated. She despises his job because she feels it competes for time with him. He won't go to church anymore because he feels he has to jockey for the passion she freely gives the church. She tires of his visions and the stuff he's trying to do. He becomes lackadaisical, ambivalent. They're both like: "Psh, whatever."

The husband buries himself in his work because he does not want to come home. Now they become weary of each other. And so, no matter how long they've been married, they wake up one morning and say, "This ain't working. You've got your thing, I've got my thing, let's just do our things separately." The loss of hope for the marriage and ministry is now the norm. And because neither wants the marriage, it dies along with their ministry.

When brokenness occurs in marriage, pain and loss always follow. Marriage is never an island of itself. There are always family members and friends who are directly and personally affected by the success or failure of any marriage. Whether or not the couple acknowledges or believes it, unknown casualties happen when they walk away from a marriage.

You don't realize it because you're focused on how you feel, what you want. You're not even thinking about how this is going to affect your son at school or how it's going to affect your daughter in the future. Because you're so focused on your unmet needs and wants, you can't see that this will affect how she sees men, how your son views women. Then you bring them to church and they have confusion because now they see you lifting your hands and giving God glory; or they see you speaking in tongues and walking around the church. Later they see you and their father cussing at each other and they can't delineate the difference between the two. Consequently they resent the very thing that was supposed to change them.

WHERE IS GOD NOW?

We have to remember that marriage is a covenant between two people and God. Scripture is specific about this because with God covenant-making was essential and unequivocal—so much so that God demonstrated it by the price of shared blood. Covenant always involved sacrifice. Jesus Christ obviously demonstrated this on the cross. We forget that it takes blood, sweat, and tears to make covenant happen. Wherever there's covenant, somebody's got to bleed for it.

> **Marriage is a covenant.**
>
> **Where there's covenant,**
>
> **somebody's got to bleed.**

So let's back up—in the name of Jesus—with this couple, before the death of the marriage. They are in this dysfunctional situation going to work, grinding, coming home, tolerating each other. They're not talking to each other 'cause they're tired and worn out. They know that people look up to them, so now they're overly concerned about image—on top of the personal and familial pressures, now they're dealing with the pressure of public scrutiny. It can be overwhelming, because now it's like living in a fishbowl. And because they're perpetrating the happy, solid couple, young adults come to them asking for relationship advice. They don't want to turn them down, but outsiders don't understand what they're dealing with privately.

LESSONS TO BE LEARNED FROM THIS SCENARIO

1. Never allow yourselves to be judged by other people who place expectations on you. Stop allowing yourself to be put on pedestals. Just be real with people about where you are! And don't let people bring their judgment on you! God needs people who are real (and so do people); who say, "Look, we're real. We got real struggles like you. But God has given us the grace to get through it."

2. The church has to be open about real issues and struggles. What blows me away are all these folk who want you to think they are top of the hierarchy or elite—better than you, like they're on some spiritual pedestal. They pretend they don't argue or have issues. No! The devil is a liar!

I don't care how much anointing you got, there's no way two people are going to come together and not have a good ol' fashioned argument every now and then. Arguments are actually healthy for relationships—if you use them correctly. Jesus and His twelve disciples had some issues and arguments with each other. Being married doesn't mean you won't ever deal with conflict. In fact, it's best to know going in that arguments will happen in a healthy marriage—it's normal. The important thing to remember is how you argue. Keep your focus on the problem. Attack the problem, not each other.

SACRIFICING MARRIAGE ON THE ALTAR OF MINISTRY—A PATHOLOGY

I've developed a model called *the pathology of sacrificing marriage on the altar of ministry and work*. The classic example is of

Moses in Exodus 18. You know how awesome Moses was as a leader, but in his marriage to Zipporah, Moses had issues. Although he was doing what God called him to do, Moses isolated himself from his own family—that was his first issue. This problem manifested itself in that he—second issue—neglected his children, who represented high marks of his testimony.

Remember, in the Hebrew Bible names meant something. As a young man Moses was running from Pharaoh after defending one of his people, a Hebrew, by killing an Egyptian. He comes to Midian and meets Jethro, who hires him to tend sheep. Soon Moses meets Zipporah, Jethro's daughter, who represents escape. They fall in love and marry. Later they have two sons: Gershom, named for an episode in Moses' life, means "I have been an alien in a strange land" (Exodus 18:3 KJV). At that point in Moses' life he felt like an alien in a strange land. His second son, Eliezer, reminded him of how the Lord helped him and delivered him from the sword of Pharaoh (v. 4).

Then one day while Moses is tending sheep, God speaks to Moses from the burning bush and gives Moses a huge assignment: to use the powers God has given him to bring God's people out of Egypt because the Egyptians are oppressing them. Moses packs up his wife and sons and they go to Egypt. And you know the story: Moses' brother, Aaron, joins him, and they appeal to Pharaoh to let God's people go. Again and again, Pharaoh refuses. God sends the ten plagues, and finally the people are set free. During this time Moses is the key leader and the people trust and depend heavily on him because they know he obeys and speaks for God.

Also during this time Moses sends Zipporah and their sons back to Midian, to her father. He sends her back. Now, that word *send* literally means divorcement or separation. When

Moses sends Zipporah back to her father, it represents his inability to incorporate her into his ministry; when he neglects his sons, he also is saying, "I am neglecting significant parts of my past."

Although he is constantly in demand managing the lives of an estimated two million people, Moses is isolated from his family, neglecting his children, marriage on the rocks. Now, Moses' father-in-law is also a priest and he has heard of the work Moses has done for the Israelites. Jethro comes into the wilderness where Moses is encamped at the mountain of God. He sends word to Moses: "I, your father-in-law Jethro, am coming to you with your wife and her two sons" (Exodus 18:6).

MINISTRY—YOUR PLACE OF ESCAPE?

Family should always be your place of escape. But rather than retreat home to escape the dragons and demands at work, you stay longer at your ministry to escape family. You tell yourself that you are in ministry, forsaking all for God, and imagine that God is pleased. You know your schedule is hectic and unrealistic; you leave home early and energetic and come home late and empty. Where is the escape?

CONSUMED BY MINISTRY IDENTITY

You are working against yourself, trying to build up the marriage while tearing it down for the "love of God." Nobody wants to deal with this in church; we just want to keep on being dysfunctional, looking like everything's fine with hallelujah and glory all around.

When Jethro comes to meet Moses, they sit and Moses tells his father-in-law:

about everything the LORD had done to Pharaoh and the Egyptians for Israel's sake and about all the hardships they had met along the way and how the LORD had saved them.

Jethro was delighted to hear about all the good things the LORD had done for Israel in rescuing them from the hand of the Egyptians. (Exodus 18:8-9 NIV)

It sounds as though Moses is testifying to what God has done in his life, but what he's really doing is bragging about all the things that have happened since he's been leading. He's consumed, his whole identity is tied around what he does. He's lost in his ministry. He's trying to convince his father-in-law because he knows Jethro has an agenda: he knew that when he learned that Jethro had brought Zipporah and the boys with him.

Like Moses, we can lose ourselves in our careers or in our service to others. With that comes the addendum of people beginning to associate us with what we do and respond to us only in that capacity. They lose the person in the ministry and forget that we are people. They forget that we like going to the movies or the games, that we like to play and have fun. We don't want to do a counseling session while we are out; we are people too. But if we allow them to respond to us only in that capacity, we've lost ourselves and enable that behavior. This happens when our conversation is all about whatever project or ministry is consuming our time. There's no separation for you.

The next day Moses took his seat to serve as judge for the people, and they stood around him from morning till evening. When his father-in-law saw all that Moses was doing for the people, he said, "What is this you are doing for the people? Why do you alone sit as judge, while all these people stand around you from morning till evening?" (vv. 13-14 NIV)

NO PRIVATE TIME

In verse 12, Moses has no private time. People are in his business. When he is sitting down and making sacrifices to God, Aaron and all the elders of Israel come to eat bread with Moses, and everybody shows up, like "Can I have a moment?" He has a distorted perception of ministry: Moses sits to judge the people and the people stand by Moses from the morning to the evening.

You need to understand, *we are not called to be Jesus Jr.* Keep letting people stretch you like that, keep letting people make you a workaholic, from the morning to the evening, from out the house at six in the morning, back

Christians are not called to be Jesus Jr.

at home at eight or nine at night, 'cause the people *need* you. Keep on because people will kill you, come to your funeral, and look at you and say, "You sure look natural." You've got to face your own need to be needed.

INFLATED SENSE OF IMPORTANCE AND MISPLACED PRIORITIES

Moses answered him, "Because the people come to me to seek God's will. Whenever they have a dispute, it is brought to me, and I decide between the parties and inform them of God's decrees and laws."

Moses' father-in-law replied, "What you are doing is not good. You and these people who come to you will only wear yourselves out. The work is too heavy for you; you cannot handle it alone. Listen now to me and

I will give you some advice, and may God be with you."
(vv. 15-19 NIV)

Moses has an inflated sense of importance. He's saying, "I do this because they need me." Can you remember your thoughts as you leave the office at 8 p.m.? Do you ask yourself why you do this? If you think it's because they need you—that you're the only one who can perform this service—try this: die! Just mentally fast-forward your death and you'll see that they'll have somebody else doing it next week.

As Moses talks to Jethro, you can see he's trying to justify his behavior. See, they have these things going on, they come to me and I judge between one and the other and I make them notice the statutes of God and His law. See, he's *I-istic*, it's all about what I do. Moses doesn't even process the idea, but he's going to have to learn how to delegate; he's got to learn that other people are qualified to do it too. And so he's overloaded and functioning in a burnout mode. He's doing so much, like some of you. You're so overloaded that you're burned-out and you're trying to function at 100 percent when your body and your mind and your spirit are at 30 percent.

Remember you've got to learn how to stay in your assignment, not burn up or go up in flames. When God called Moses out of the burning bush, the bush was on fire but the fire didn't consume the bush. Whatever is your ministry/ assignment/work, it should never burn you up. Every ministry or job should have a burning prohibition: when you feel burned-out, know that you're out of order. If you are burning out, you need help. God never meant for you to go it alone in your ministry. Like Moses, God wants you to accept help and lean on God's power to accomplish your goals.

BURNED-OUT

We think when people bring us stuff that it is urgent, that it's important. But we have to discern what is urgent and what is not. Sometimes people bring issues to you as though they are of extreme urgency and later you find out they were blowing the issue out of proportion. They call, saying, "It's urgent, can you call me back?" And you call them back, and they say, "What was the score last night?" How can that be urgent? See, when they say urgent, that's not always the case. So, verse 17 says, "Moses' father-in-law said to him, 'The thing that you do is not good' "—man, you burning yourself out, you going to wear away, and watch this, not just you—there's collateral damage involved in this, 'cause the people that are with you, they gonna be tired too.

This operation is too heavy for you. You are not able to perform this by yourself, nor were you meant to. If you are stressed, then you distress people who serve you and with you. So everybody's stressed now, isn't that amazing? In some companies and workplaces, even in some churches, you walk in and everybody's tense, because everybody's so stressed.

A QUIET PLACE CALLED LOVE

How do you nurture your relationship in the midst of work, play, friends, family, alone-time, and even time spent doing the Lord's work? Here's a starting point that I have used. This would be a good text to send to your spouse; just send anytime because it's a blessing: "There's a quiet place I found. I know we got commitments and we got work. We're working, grinding; dealing with bills and obligations; flying across the country. We've got calendars and children, we've got this and that, but I found this quiet place and it's called Love. I'll meet you there."

EIGHT PRINCIPLES TO BALANCE YOUR RELATIONSHIP

Here are eight principles to help you balance and nurture your relationship. Because if you put in the kind of investment it takes to forge a long-lasting, committed relationship, you won't want to throw it away or ignore it. Like you and your spouse, your relationship has needs and desires. Just like there are individual needs on a team, there are also team needs. You need kindness and acceptance; your relationship needs faithfulness and for you to spend quality time together. If you can do that, your relationship will point you toward the glory of God and you will find blessing in your marriage.

1. APPRECIATE YOUR SPOUSE'S QUALITIES

Learn to appreciate and enjoy the way God made your partner. Celebrate your differences as special components that make the two of you more complete. The differences between the two of you may be in personality, gifts, types, talents, even seasons of life. Whatever they are, learn to benefit from the differences. Naturally, you will have different gifts and functions within society, community, family, church; but your hearts should remain intertwined. Not collapsed into each other, but connected in an intimate way.

Your relationship will mature as you recognize that the other likes this, while I thrive on that. Those differences should not be points of conflict but points of growth. As your marriage grows stronger, you learn to complement, not fight against, one other. You know there's value in appreciating your differences. The various ways you both serve and move in the world make you stronger as a couple. You both begin to understand the qualities of the person God has given you to be with to celebrate your potential.

2. DON'T COMPARE

Don't compare your spouse's gifts with those of someone else of a similar capacity. You can't ask her, "Why you don't act like his wife?" Brother, I'd duck if I were you, 'cause you're about to get hurt. "Why you don't treat me like so-and-so treats his wife?" Sister, that statement just might get you in deep trouble. Never compare your mate to anyone. Don't create unrealistic templates for your partner. You will have these models in your mind of what you think ought to be, but the way to approach that is not by comparing. Whatever you do, don't compare them with your Mom or Dad.

When we create and buy into these templates, they do nothing but work against the very thing we're trying to achieve.

3. HONOR ONE ANOTHER

Ephesians 5:21 tells us to "submit to one another out of reverence for Christ" (NIV). Paul then proceeds to tell the wives to submit to and respect their husbands and husbands to love their wives. Humility is important. When you come home there is a co-submission. See, you got to check your work, your title, your position of authority at the door. Yes, you have titles; you're the boss on your job, but you can't bring that persona to your home. You have to drop the boss attitude when you come home because there is no hierarchy in the home. You may be the principal at school, but at home you're wifey or hubby. You can't treat your husband the way you treat the students or your co-workers. At home you should welcome the opportunity to just be yourself with your boo. Honor your spouse with the love and tenderness you want to receive, and thank God you have a sanctuary where you can be yourself and be loved for who you are.

Also be aware that sometimes what makes you successful at work will make you a failure at home. Doug is a successful plant manager. He has worked his way to the top of the company, in part because he is accurate and detail-orientated. He has a reputation for not letting a project go out the door unless is it just right. At home, Doug was driving his wife and children crazy being the same way he was at work. Running down every last detail made him a dependable go-to person at work, but at home he just seemed controlling and perfectionistic and never satisfied with anything his family did. Doug had to learn to be more flexible and to adapt in his relationships at home.

4. BE LOYAL

In Genesis 12:1 God makes Abraham a promise. He says that He will make Abraham a great nation, and later God promises Abraham that He will bless those who bless him. Abraham, the Bible says, "got up in obedience to God, and he took Sarah his wife with him."

It's important to understand how to be loyal. Loyalty is about your heart. Proverbs 4:23 reminds us, "Keep your heart with all diligence, / For out of it spring the issues of life." The lesson is to be careful what you let in your heart. And loyalty between spouses is huge. Seasoned couples know how to remain friends and fight for each other. Their relationship is like a football game; they spend time in the huddle working out the plays, designing the game plan. Often we allow the enemy to make us believe that our spouses don't get it.

When God gave Abraham a vision, he took his wife with him. He did not leave her behind. That was the mistake Moses made. Abraham did not leave Sarah behind, because he knew whatever God was going to do through him, his business, or his vision, that provision included Sarah and without her it would not happen.

5. CHERISH THE INTIMACY IN YOUR MARRIAGE

We should always have enough energy for each other to have meaningful and undistracted intimacy. In Titus 2:4 the Bible says that wives should love their husbands. It says the older women should "teach the young women to be sober, to love their husbands, to love their children" (KJV). Here is how the mature women ought to begin: "Baby, come here. Let me tell you how to . . ." Seasoned couples have many stories and rich histories to share with new couples. They can tell young adults how to maintain the energy it takes to have meaningful and undistracted intimacy. Common sense says that we have to be in-to-each-other to achieve intimacy. That means we can't be in the bed with cell phones sending text messages. If while you're in bed you hear, "Hold on for a minute, I got to check e-mail," something is really wrong. Protect the intimacy in the marriage by creating some loving rules that support creating private and romantic spaces and times for you and your mate.

6. BE SPIRITUALLY ATTENTIVE TO ONE ANOTHER

Learn to draw from each other's spiritual potential. Remember that pressure can stifle personal sharing in this area. Maintain boundaries. Don't allow ministry or work to pull you away from sacred family commitments. Set priorities and articulate them to the people you work with and to the church.

Hebrews 12:1 tells you to lose all the weight and sin that besets you and run with patience the race set before you. You got to set boundaries around your relationship. You can't be counseling on your vacation because you got a project due. You got to set some boundaries. I know pastors who haven't had vacations in years, and when they finally get out in the water, miles away from the church, the cell phone rings and, "Pastor, can you come back and do the funeral?" I know how it goes. Everybody needs some time away. For example, you know it's your anniversary with your wife and you've got all this stuff planned. Then here comes somebody pulling you away, "I just need; I just need to talk to somebody; I just need to talk to you." You say, "Well, let me just go and get this, I'll be a little late." You got to have Sabbaths. You got to set aside some days where it's just you.

7. LEARN HOW TO RECONNECT

When I open up the Bible, I'm like any of you, I need to hear a word from the Lord. But because the Bible is like a manual for my job, sometimes it's difficult for me to separate the work of preparing for a sermon and the joy of hearing God speak to me through His Word. I have to pray, "Lord, speak to me without giving me a word for them." I have to intentionally disconnect from the flock I'm leading, to re-connect with God, my Father.

I had to learn how to step away and have moments of med-itation, just walking in the park or going down to the coffee shop and just sitting and opening up books and spending time reconnecting, because I was getting lost in what I was doing. Again, Hebrews 12:1 says, "lay aside every weight, and the sin which so easily ensnares us, and let us run with en-durance the race that is set before us." It says, "Lay aside every weight, and the sin which so easily besets us." Sin is missing the mark. I was missing the mark, working so hard, consumed, and losing me in the process.

You can also lose your relationship if you don't take time to reconnect with each other. Yes, sometimes it will have to be planned. If you have to, set an appointment with your spouse. But surprise her with something that says, *I've been thinking about you today.*

8. MAKE HAPPY MEMORIES—
HAVE FUN WITH YOUR SPOUSE

Too many couples forget how essential humor is to keep-ing the mood light in your home. Let happiness be your focus. Strive—without making it too hard—to make the main atmosphere in your home a happy, positive, safe, welcoming, friendly zone. One mistake married people and even single people make with their relationships is forgetting how to play. Think about this: when you sit down with your husband or wife and you have a conversation, take note of what percentage of the conversation is about you and what percentage is about work or the kids. If it's more about work or the kids than about you personally, then take that as a warning. Talk about work and what you do usually does not include information about who you are. It's all about the business. Who can have fun with that? Going on and on about the issues at work and bills and managing the home makes it hard to have fun. Your conversations become boring:

You: How was your day?
Her: Blah blah blah. Did you pay that bill?
You: Yep.
Her: OK, good.
You: Good. What's to eat?
Her: That was good.
You: OK, good. All right, good night.

Soon you feel a distance growing. You don't really know what's going on between you. You feel your relationship changing and you're wondering what God is showing you— not about work or church—just about you, the person. When you are so tied to the details and demands of work or church, you begin to miss out on living. You no longer feel you're connected to the human race. You're so tied to all this stuff and all of a sudden, twenty years have slipped by and you feel you don't know each other anymore. You grow apart because you stopped communicating about twenty years ago. You were talking about the things, but not about you. Stop for a moment and just do something fun together.

CONCLUSION

This book gives you five steps in the journey of getting together and staying together. I hope you see that a long-lasting, fulfilling, intimate relationship is a beautiful thing, something worth working on and fighting for. In anyone's life it's not the number of important meetings or how much stuff you have piled up in the closet. It's not the amount of sports equipment or number of designer dresses; it is about lasting love, the kind that God wants you to have.

To be successful as a couple, you must center your relationship in God's purpose and be ready for a holy hookup, meet the standard, be real, be on the same team, and live to the glory of God.

Now here is a blessing for you.

May God bless you with all the exquisite joys of loving that special someone. May you find wholeness and peace with Jesus, who is able to present you faultless before the throne of God. May you see yourself and your spouse as valuable children of God. And may you find love and find it loving one another. Amen.

THINK ABOUT THIS

1. Describe a time when someone sacrificed something for you or when you sacrificed something for someone else.

2. Ever thought of Moses being so swamped at work that he sends his wife and sons back to her parents? Even when you are doing good for the Lord, your priorities can get lost

or mixed up. Do you know when to say no? Do you need to be needed?

3. Discuss the temptations that go along with having an inflated sense of importance. Are there warning signals that let us know that is happening? Discuss the temptations that lead to being burned out.

4. Share some ideas that can help couples keep the romance in the relationship and create happy memories.